Teach®
Yourself

Correct English

B.A. Phythian

First revised by Albert Rowe
This edition revised by Ron Simpson

For UK order enquiries: please contact Bookpoint Ltd,
130 Milton Park, Abingdon, Oxon OX14 4SB.
Telephone: +44 (0) 1235 827720. *Fax:* +44 (0) 1235 400454.
Lines are open 09.00–17.00, Monday to Saturday, with a 24-hour
message answering service. Details about our titles and how to
order are available at www.teachyourself.com

For USA order enquiries: please contact McGraw-Hill Customer
Services, PO Box 545, Blacklick, OH 43004-0545, USA.
Telephone: 1-800-722-4726. *Fax:* 1-614-755-5645.

For Canada order enquiries: please contact McGraw-Hill Ryerson
Ltd, 300 Water St, Whitby, Ontario L1N 9B6, Canada.
Telephone: 905 430 5000. *Fax:* 905 430 5020.

Long renowned as the authoritative source for self-guided learning –
with more than 50 million copies sold worldwide – the **Teach Yourself**
series includes over 500 titles in the fields of
languages, crafts, hobbies, business, computing and education.

British Library Cataloguing in Publication Data: a catalogue record
for this title is available from the British Library.

Library of Congress Catalog Card Number: on file.

First published in UK 1985 by Hodder Education, part of Hachette UK,
338 Euston Road, London NW1 3BH.

First published in US 1985 by The McGraw-Hill Companies, Inc.

This edition published 2010.

Previously published as *Teach Yourself Good English* and *Teach Yourself
Correct English*

The **Teach Yourself** name is a registered trade mark of Hodder Headline.

Copyright © 1985 B.A. Phythian

Revisions and additional material © 2000, 2003 Albert Rowe

© 2010 Ron Simpson

Typeset by MPS Limited, A Macmillan Company.

Printed in Great Britain for Hodder Education, an Hachette UK Company,
338 Euston Road, London NW1 3BH, by CPI Cox & Wyman, Reading,
Berkshire RG1 8EX.

The publisher has used its best endeavours to ensure that the URLs for
external websites referred to in this book are correct and active at the time of
going to press. However, the publisher and the author have no responsibility
for the websites and can make no guarantee that a site will remain live or
that the content will remain relevant, decent or appropriate.

Hachette UK's policy is to use papers that are natural, renewable and
recyclable products and made from wood grown in sustainable forests.
The logging and manufacturing processes are expected to conform to the
environmental regulations of the country of origin.

Impression number   10 9 8 7 6 5 4 3 2 1

Year   2014 2013 2012 2011 2010

Acknowledgements

The author and publishers are grateful to the following for
permission to reproduce copyright material in this book:

Malcolm Bradbury: one extract (p. 153) from *Who Do You Think
You Are?* reproduced by permission of the author and Martin
Secker and Warburg Ltd; Glenda Cooper and the *Independent*:
one extract (p. 176) from the article 'Idolising rock stars can be
bad for your health' of 4th April 1997; William Golding: one
extract (p. 161) from *Lord of the Flies* reprinted by permission of
Faber and Faber Ltd, London, and also reprinted by permission
of the Putman Publishing Group, New York. Copyright © 1954
by William Gerald Golding, renewed 1982; Ernest Hemingway:
one extract (p. 160) from *A Farewell to Arms*, copyright 1929
Charles Scribner's Sons' copyright renewed © 1957, reprinted
with permission of Charles Scribner's Sons, New York, and also
reprinted with permission of Jonathan Cape Ltd, London, and the
Executors of the Ernest Hemingway Estate; Simon Hoggart: one
extract (p. 152) from *On the House* reproduced by permission
of the author and Robson Books Ltd; Laurie Lee: one extract
(p. 159) from *Cider with Rosie* reproduced by permission of the
author and The Hogarth Press; Thomas Mann: one extract (p. 164)
from *Death in Venice* reproduced by permission of the author
and Martin Secker and Warburg Ltd, London, and also reprinted
by permission of Alfred A. Knopf, Inc, New York, from *Death in
Venice and Seven Other Stories*, translated by H. T. Lowe-Porter;
Angela Neustatter and The *Guardian*: one extract (p. 179) from
the article 'Mum, I hardly missed you'; Suzanne Moore and the
Independent: one extract (p. 177) from the article 'Too many
'ologists make you boring' of 4th April 1997; William Sansom:
one extract (p. 174) from *Christmas* © 1968 by William Sansom;
Dylan Thomas: two extracts (pp. 149, 150) from *A Prospect of
the Sea* reproduced by permission of the author and Dent;
James Vance Marshall: one extract (p. 162) from *Walkabout*

Credits

Contents

Only got a minute?

Correct English is built around understanding the accurate use of two central parts of speech: the noun and the verb. If we go back to the origins of speech, the first necessities are to identify people, animals or things (nouns) and say what they are doing or suffering (verb). If we take such imaginary first statements as 'We eat food' or 'Hunters kill animals', 'eat' and 'kill' are verbs, the other words are nouns, except for 'we'.

'We' is an example of how verbs and nouns can be central to understanding other parts of speech. It is an example of a pronoun, a word used instead of a noun. When we add in words that tell us more about nouns (adjectives) and words that tell us more about verbs (adverbs), we have five of the basic parts of speech.

Other parts of speech (prepositions and conjunctions) are concerned with linking together shorter units of words into a sentence – and, when we look at sentences, we again realise that nouns and verbs are primary. A sentence must have a finite verb, one that relates to a period of time (past, present or future) and it must have a subject (a noun or noun equivalent) unless it's a command. A sentence may contain much more, but these elements are the only essential ones.

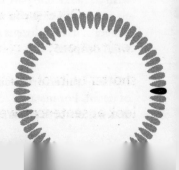

5 Only got five minutes?

English is a notoriously illogical and inconsistent language. What are you to do with a language where 'tough' rhymes with 'snuff', but not with 'though' or 'through'? Or one which normally forms the past tense and participle by adding '-ed' or '-t', but produces such oddities as 'is', 'was' and 'been', and 'go', 'went' and 'gone'? Or one which makes a habit of creating perplexing homophones (words sounding the same) such as 'there', 'their' and 'they're' and ignoring spelling rules at every opportunity?

However, it's important to remember that spelling is only a tool; it is not the most essential feature of correct English. Good spelling is highly desirable, but, with spellcheck facilities, it is possible to write good English whilst struggling with spelling. It is not possible to write good English without grasping the basics of sentence construction, English idioms and the subtleties of register.

Sentences begin in simplicity. 'The sun shone' is a simple subject-finite verb construct. We can add many extras and still preserve the simple sentence format: 'In the month of July, on the Fylde coast more famous for its blustery winds and sudden showers, the sun shone on 24 days out of 31.' The essential element of a sentence is a finite verb, so, when we wish to add more of those, we have to turn the sentence into something more complicated. Such sentences are joined together by conjunctions: 'The sun shone *and* the wind dropped'. Here the two halves are equal, but sometimes you will wish to make one part the main clause, the other a subordinate clause. In this case you use a subordinating conjunction ('as', 'when', 'where', 'if' and dozens of others): '*When* the sun came out, the wind dropped'.

Many of the errors committed by writers of English are errors of detail. For instance, one of the major difficulties for speakers and writers of English as a foreign language is with the choice of prepositions. The difference between 'The box is *on* the table' and 'The box is *under* the table' is obvious, but there are more subtle distinctions and it is important to know which preposition goes with which noun, verb and adjective. For instance, 'bored' must be followed by 'with' or 'by', not 'of', and 'different to/from/than' is a recurring problem.

The idiomatic use of English often requires you to distinguish between very similar words. Some pairs of words pose a particular problem because they have distinct meanings but can be used for the same thing. If a teacher or interviewer gives an exercise which depends upon reading something to the class and checking understanding, is that an 'oral' test (spoken, not written) or an 'aural' test (checking that it has been correctly heard and understood)? In this situation, meaning overlaps, but the words are as different as 'mouth' and 'ears'. Such confusions can easily affect even respectable publications. Recently, quality newspapers and journals have suddenly found difficulty in distinguishing 'principle' (an idea or a moral stance that guides our actions) from 'principal' (meaning 'main' or anybody who is the main person, such as the principal of a college).

Writing correct English also requires an awareness of register: the tone of your writing. There is no single correct register. You need to consider whether you are imparting facts (remove any personal reference, clear organization essential) or attempting to persuade (consider the emotional effect of your words, allow your opinions to emerge). Perhaps you are engaged on an imaginative or creative piece, with much more use of metaphors – writing that can please for its own sake, not just as a vehicle for the subject matter. Perhaps you are submitting a report or a request to some higher authority where a touch too much familiarity could be your undoing. Even (perhaps, especially) in the age of emails, control of register is essential to good English.

Part one
Words and sentences

1

English today

In this chapter you will learn:
- *about standard English and modern English*
- *idioms and colloquial language*
- *about accent.*

Standard English

Over the past hundred years, a standard form of the English language has evolved that today is used throughout the world by many millions of people. Known as standard English, it is the variety of English taught in the educational systems of the English-speaking world. It is also taught to students in those parts of the world where, increasingly, English is the second language, such as India, Kenya, Nigeria and Singapore. Spoken and written by people of social and political prestige, its use – even with the differences of vocabulary, accent and idiom peculiar to different parts of the world – ensures the understanding of the widest possible audience.

Standard English is the written English of the business letter, the official report, most serious novels and the leader columns of broadsheet newspapers, and the spoken English of the job interview and the television documentary. It is not necessarily stiff or dignified, though these qualities may be needed at times. Rather it is the language used when the occasion requires a degree of formality or when one wants to be easily understood by strangers. It can be spoken in any accent.

English in the world

The standard English that we know today began as the East Midlands dialect used by Chaucer in the fourteenth century in his *Canterbury Tales*. This form of English acquired great social and political prestige and became the basis of modern English from about the fifteenth century onwards, as English political power and influence developed and spread throughout the world. Modern English is the result of a constantly changing process of development and enrichment from other cultures as well as our own: from languages such as French and Latin, but also from elsewhere in the world and – particularly in the twentieth and twenty-first centuries – from American English. It is a characteristic of the English language that it has absorbed so many words and expressions from abroad. These sometimes co-exist with older native expressions, and often become so familiar that we do not recognize them as foreign (see Chapter 10).

The impetus for standardization has, however, always competed with determined localizing forces. Universal education and the spread of standard English may sadly have pushed some minor dialects to extinction, but others have nonetheless survived, for example, London Cockney and Liverpool Scouse, which retain their particular vocabularies and grammars. Nowadays, there is perhaps an increased respect for the English spoken by certain social or ethnic groups, such as pidgin, Caribbean creole, Black English and Indian English, both within the UK and elsewhere in the world.

Insight

Accent and dialect are often confused. Different regional accents are still strongly with us, and are more acceptable by the year for newsreaders, radio and television reporters, presenters, etc., but a true dialect implies distinction of vocabulary and grammar. Growing up in the Black Country, I regularly heard the 'bin' and 'bist' of Old English, but this usage is no longer current. The 'thees' and 'thas' of Yorkshire remain, but increasingly dialects are adopted on the basis of age and social groupings, not region.

There has always been a strong tradition of novelists (from Sir Walter Scott to Irving Welsh) and poets (Robert Burns and Rudyard Kipling) writing in the spoken language, or making their characters speak with particular dialects. Many poets and novelists writing today use their own varieties of English:

Richard's Brother Speaks
Richard ...
What's the matter? Why you smilin' no more?
You wretch, you bruk the window.
Daddy a go peel you 'kin,
'im a go peel it like he peel orange.
When Daddy come tru dat door,
You better run.
You better leave de country!
'im a go peel you 'kin.
You bottom a go warm tonight though!
Me goin' cook dinner pon you back side
When 'im done wid you.
Richard, 'im come!
Run, bwoy, run!

Desmond Strachen

Some varieties, such as pidgin, have moved a long way from their English roots. They often use a simplified form of grammar which, for example, does away with complicated irregular verbs such as 'to be'. Sometimes a language is so far removed from standard English in the words and expressions used, and in its grammar and pronunciation, that its speakers are able to use it as a kind of secret code that excludes others from their discussion; this has happened with Jamaican creole. Sometimes the more academic standard English taught in schools co-exists with a very different kind of spoken language, as in Indian English, which has acquired words from other native Indian languages (*lakh* = a sum of money, *goonda* = a hooligan), invents new phrases (*gunnybag* = sack), mixes Indian and English expressions (*newspaper wallah* = man who sells newspapers), and has a wonderfully inventive line in insults and politenesses.

More recently, there are signs that in some developing countries the spoken form of English is achieving a respectability that makes standard English seem somewhat old-fashioned and out of touch and, curiously, it may well be shown at some point in the future that these 'living' languages have followed much the same development path away from standard English as that of the modern European languages away from Latin.

Modern trends

Changes in the character of the language in the last 100 years mirror the enormous social and political changes which have taken place over the same period. There is now as much informality in the use of English as there is in social life. Those whose business it is to communicate with us – politicians, journalists and broadcasters – now use language which is much more informal and accessible than used to be the case. At one time 'good' English was identified by a rather high-flown and artificial style thought to be suitable for public occasions and official correspondence, and was spoken with an exaggerated 'public school' accent (*a gel who's fraffly good at goff*); now it is felt to lie in a more natural tone of voice. This trend has been reflected in novels, plays and poems, which are now written in a language much closer to the people than the more 'literary' style of the early twentieth century. One result of this popularizing trend is that the everyday user of written English may sometimes find it difficult to differentiate between good standard English needed as a tool for the job or for other specific purposes and the more colloquial, everyday forms of the language.

One has only to listen to television chat shows or be aware of how one talks to one's friends and colleagues, or to analyse the language of emails, to notice the very different type of English we use every day. We talk in a kind of verbal shorthand, making use of colloquial expressions, repeating ourselves, not finishing our sentences. This is not necessarily bad English, although it sometimes is: bad English is incorrect, unclear, long-winded or pretentious, and there are plenty of examples of each in the language of the mass media. Words chatter out at us every day, and we have to be on our guard not to let the language become impoverished.

English idioms

English has a rich store of phrases which through their construction are peculiar to the language and have become characteristic of general usage. Known as idioms, these phrases are figurative; that is, they are imaginative and not to be taken literally, although most of them had a literal meaning originally. Figurative expressions of this kind are drawn from our common experience in many different fields of human activity:

seafaring (*on the rocks, left high and dry*); fishing (*trawl for business, hook, line and sinker*); agriculture (*plough a straight furrow, crop up*); warfare (*hold your fire, cross swords with*); the theatre (*play to the gallery, bring the house down*); gardening (*weed out, a thorny problem*); the Bible (*the salt of the earth, Good Samaritan*); crime (*caught red-handed, enough rope to hang him by*); trades (*jack of all trades, other irons in the fire*); cooking (*out of the frying pan into the fire, gone off the boil*); music (*play second fiddle, blow one's own trumpet*); sport (*keep your eye on the ball, a good innings*).

There are hundreds of others. The Authorized Version of the Bible, in particular, is a very rich source of common idioms.

English idioms sometimes defy logic and the rules of grammar. Certain words, often small words such as prepositions, have very different meanings in different expressions and can be puzzling to the foreigner. No native speaker is likely to be puzzled by the number of idioms using the word *turn*: they include *down, in, off, on, out, over, round, to, up, against, about*, and *away*. But a foreigner may be forgiven for being bewildered that *down* and *up* sometimes express direction as in *turn up the hill, turn down one's collar* but not in *turn up at the party*; that there are colloquial meanings for *turn on* (excite) and *turn off* (cause to lose interest); that *turn in* may mean *go to bed, hand in* or *fold inwards. Turn out* is logical in *turn out the drawers*, but less so in *it's turned out nice again*. Idiom dictates that we are '*at* a loss', but '*in* a quandary', '*out* of sorts' but '*in* low spirits', 'aware *of*' but 'alert *to*', '*on* our guard' but '*at* the ready'.

Despite their homely flavour, these are standard English usages, not colloquialisms, and provide a constant source of interest to the student of English. However, the danger is that if overused, once-colourful expressions may grow pale, losing their power and most of their sense. Some phrases lose their original connections to such an extent that they become mixed up in use. We may read of a traffic bottleneck which needs to be *reduced*, or *ironed out*, instead of widened; of a milestone that is *broken* or *overtaken* instead of passed, or of a project such as the Millennium Wheel which has finally *taken off*. Some popular images become devalued into clichés: *blueprint, fine-tooth comb, track record, acid test, springboard* – everyone has their favourite examples (see Chapter 10). In this way many serviceable expressions pass through cliché into ridicule through overuse and failure of imagination.

Many widely used and colourful phrases may be defended on the grounds that they are more concise and no more objectionable than their alternatives: for example, *fall between two stools, thin end of the wedge, swings and roundabouts, white elephant, in a nutshell, high and dry*. Some people would feel, however, that these expressions are better suited to the spoken than the written language.

Colloquial language

It is only compilers of dictionaries who are obliged to define which words are colloquial (conversational) or slang, and it is often a matter of judgement to decide whether a word is sufficiently informal to be regarded as colloquial rather than standard English. The problem is compounded by the fluidity of the language: words often come into the language as slang – *boss, mob,* or *rock* (music), for example – and with the passage of time acquire respectability. Other words remain colloquial, or drop out of the language altogether. However, we tend to speak rather more colloquially than we write, and it is usually possible to identify language which is better spoken than written. Look at some of the expressions we use in everyday speech which on the whole we would not use when writing formally (although we might well do so in an informal letter or when using email):

> *great*/wonderful; *cool*/fashionable; *grotty*/unpleasantly dirty, shabby; *like a dream*/exactly as one would want; *get it, get the message*/understand; *chill out*/calm down; *clean up*/make a big profit; *throw*/disconcert; *dump*/abandon or a run-down place; *send up*/mock or mimic; *rip off*/defraud; *grab*/appeal to; *nick*/ steal; *wind up*/taunt or tease; *grouch*/complaint or complain; *curl up*/writhe with embarrassment; *blow up*/lose one's temper; *booze-up*/drinking session.

The margin between colloquial language and slang is very narrow,
but if a word is extreme or colourful we call it slang. It is the
most informal type of language and is used only among friends
and acquaintances, often in closed circles like the armed forces
and schools, in strongly regional dialects such as Cockney and
in occupational groups such as the criminal fraternity. Vivid and
vigorous, it is often obscene or vulgar and it produces a raw, pictorial
type of English. Slang words often have short lives as they pass in
and out of fashion. Here are a few reasonably current examples:

> money: *dough, readies, bread, lolly, bucks*; food: *nosh, grub,
> chow*; being drunk: *canned, smashed, plastered, legless, gone,
> pissed, blotto.*

You will doubtless be able to add others. As the language stands
at present, these words are not acceptable as standard English,
although it would be rash to assert that none of them will ever
become so.

Accent

We all speak English with an accent – which stems from the region
and social class of our birth, although we can and often do change
our accent as a result of the regional and social mobility nowadays
available to us. At one time, Received Pronunciation (RP) was the

only accent used by radio and television presenters, but in recent years RP has lost its monopoly. Its tone has become modified and a variety of regional accents are commonly heard in the media. The accent we use need bear no relation to the correctness of our language, but it is still the case, even nowadays, that some accents are considered 'better' than others. Edinburgh Scottish and Dublin Irish are thought to be superior to the accents of Glasgow and Liverpool. The user of RP usually finds it easier than the speaker with a pronounced regional accent to negotiate his way through a job interview or assert his legal or civil rights.

It is only comparatively recently, since the beginning of the twentieth century, that people have felt the need to adopt an accent in order to be accepted by a particular social group. Nowadays it is even quite common to have one accent for work and another for home – a kind of multi-accent approach. It is also interesting that a number of modern politicians and celebrities take great care not to let their speech seem too 'plummy' and thereby give the impression that they are out of touch with the people.

Who, what and why?

The knack of using English well, in both the written and the spoken language, is to suit it to the occasion. We need to be aware of who we are talking to, what we want to say and why – all of which should influence the kind of language we use. It is important, for instance, to be able to differentiate between words and expressions which are acceptable in any circumstances and those which are more colloquial – and may belong at least at present only to the spoken language. It is also important to understand our reason for writing or speaking. Are we trying to inform or instruct? Are we writing about something with specialist knowledge? Are we trying to sell something or persuade someone of our views? Are we telling a story? All these factors affect the way we express ourselves.

Have fun with language!

1 *Think of five expressions in general use which have their origins in one or more of the following spheres of activity:*
   a *the sea and seafaring*
   b *the land and agriculture*
   c *a sport such as football or cricket*
   d *The Bible*

2 *When talking to friends what words might you use for the following?*
   a *the police*
   b *drink*

3 *Can you think of three words used in English which may have come from each of the following countries?*
   a *America*
   b *Spain*
   c *France*
   d *Germany*

Now look them up in a good dictionary and check their country of origin. (You'll also find some in Chapter 10.)

10 THINGS TO REMEMBER

1 *English is a world language and therefore takes many forms. Every one of these is correct in a suitable context.*

2 *It is not tautological to speak of British English – though we may find the term English English odd – to distinguish it from American English and the many other dialects and forms of the English language throughout the world.*

3 *What is taken to be good English (written or spoken) changes with time.*

4 *The one definite unchanging feature of good written or spoken English is that it must be widely intelligible. English that is understood only by people in a certain region or experts in a scientific field has its place, of course, but within specific limits.*

5 *Natural use of the language is called idiomatic. There are many established idioms that are familiar to a native speaker.*

6 *Some of these idioms are tired and old and have lost their freshness and it is better to avoid them.*

7 *Colloquial language, essentially, is that of conversation, not writing. Slang is colloquial language that is one stage further from written correctness.*

8 *Increasing informality and the use of emails mean that colloquial English can be used much more widely in writing now. However, it helps to consider the situation and the relationship between writer and reader.*

9 *It is helpful to distinguish between dialect, which has its own grammatical forms and vocabulary, and accent, which is a matter merely of pronunciation.*

10 *In all aspects of modern English it is as unhelpful to allow snobbery to intrude as it is to follow the latest trends blindly.*

2

How words work

In this chapter you will learn:
- *how to use nouns, pronouns, adjectives, verbs, adverbs, prepositions and conjunctions*
- *about interjections and exclamations*
- *about words that have more than one function.*

If you want to have some knowledge of the machinery of language, it is useful to be able to understand the various different sorts of words and how they function.

Some words have simple functions (for example, describing or saying what happened) whereas others can be used for many different ones. Look at the word *round* in the following examples:

> a round building; the third round of the match; come round for a chat.

In each case *round* is performing a different function (describing an object, naming, specifying how an action is performed). Words are assigned to categories according to these functions, and these categories are called parts of speech or word classes. Following is an overview of the parts of speech.

Nouns

A noun is a naming word, from the Latin *nomen* (name).

It may name a specific person, creature, place or object (proper noun):

> William Shakespeare, Spot, Edinburgh, the *Independent*.

It may name an individual belonging to a class of people, animals or things that can be directly seen, heard, touched or smelt (common noun):

> doctor, rabbit, house, bicycle, water, squeak, stink.

It may be a quality, state of mind, attitude, idea or action that does not refer directly to the senses (abstract noun):

> intelligence, sorrow, laziness, democracy, philosophy, violence.

It may refer to a group of individual people or animals (collective noun):

> army, audience, chorus, flock, family, jury, majority, queue.

Nouns are either singular – referring to one only:

> tree, woman, quality

or plural – more than one:

> trees, women, qualities.

....
Insight
The three examples immediately above are good illustrations of different ways of forming the plural. The most common
(Contd)

method is to add 's' (*trees*), but, when the singular ends in '-y' following a consonant, '-y' becomes '-ies' (*qualities*). However, many common words form their plural irregularly, changing a vowel in the singular form (*women*). It's also worth noting that some nouns are unchanged in the plural – *sheep*, *deer* – and that nouns ending in a sibilant add an extra 'e': *masses*, *coaches*, *flashes*.

Pronouns

A pronoun stands in place of a noun: *she*, *we*, *it*, *everybody*.

Pronouns are a handy device for avoiding the repetition of nouns. Instead of writing:

The tree has been felled. The tree had been damaged in a storm,

we are able to write:

The tree has been felled. *It* had been damaged in a storm.

Pronouns may be singular (*I*, *he*, *she*, *it*) or plural (*we*, *they*); the pronoun *you* may be singular or plural depending on whether it refers to one person or to several.

The most important categories of pronoun are:

▶ **personal** e.g. I, me; you; he, she, it, him, her; we, us; they, them;
▶ **possessive** e.g. mine, his, hers, yours;
▶ **demonstrative** e.g. this, these, that, those (as in *This belonged to my father*);
▶ **interrogative** e.g. who, whose, which, what (as in *Who did that?*);
▶ **indefinite** e.g. anybody, none, no one, either, each;
▶ **relative** e.g. who, whose, what, whom, that;
▶ **reflexive** e.g. myself, ourselves, yourself, itself, himself.

Demonstrative pronouns take the same form as demonstrative adjectives. When used in place of a noun, they are demonstrative pronouns; when used to support a noun, they are demonstrative adjectives. Hence, 'That is really boring' (pronoun) and 'That book is really boring' (adjective).

Relative pronouns are so called because, as well as acting as pronouns, they relate or join groups of words. Instead of writing:

The tree has been felled. The tree (*or* It) had been damaged in a storm.

We may write:

The tree, *which* had been damaged in a storm, has been felled.

thus joining two short sentences into one by using a relative pronoun.

Adjectives

An adjective is often said to describe a noun. In fact it modifies a noun, tells us something more precise about it, though many adjectives are, indeed, descriptive:

enthusiastic, tallest, invisible.

Others give different sorts of information:

eighth, many, those.

Adjectives are normally placed before the nouns they describe (*several large white whales*) but other positions are possible:

The morning was *misty* and *cold*.
The morning, *misty* and *cold*, depressed his spirits.

If adjectives are formed from proper nouns they have capital letters (the *American* way of life, the *Christian* religion).

It is a particular flexibility of English that nouns are often used as adjectives (*alarm* clock, *police* van, *chicken* soup).

COMPARISON OF ADJECTIVES

When comparing only two persons or things, use the *-er* form of the adjective:

> Simon is *taller* than his sister.
> Which is *newer*, this one or that one?

When the adjective has no *-er* form, and in some cases to avoid clumsiness, use *more*:

> That kitten is *more active* than this one.
> His collection is *more interesting* than hers.

When comparing three or more, use the *-est* form:

> Leroy is the *tallest* of the three.
> The *tiniest* puppy is the *prettiest*.

When the adjective has no *-est* form, use *most*:

> She is by far the *most determined* of all.
> This is by far the *most sensible* of your proposals.

Verbs

A verb expresses an action or state of being: *walk, made, fought, seems, existed.*

He *mended* the puncture, *smiled, mounted* his bicycle and
  rode away.
We *are* very sad because they *have suffered* so much.
The garden *had been neglected* and the house *was ruined*.

In the first sentence, the four verbs are functioning on their own.
In the other two examples, they need to be helped by the auxiliary
verbs *to be* and *to have* in their various forms: *have, had been* and
was. There is more on verbs in Chapter 3.

Adverbs

Adverbs describe or enlarge the meaning of a verb, adjective or
other adverb.

He called *loudly*.
There was a *very* faint reply.
He called *more* loudly.

When an adverb describes a verb, it usually indicates *how, when,
where* or *why* the action of the verb is taking place.

▶ Adverbs that indicate *how* are often formed from adjectives.
▶ Usually one adds -*ly*: slow > *slowly*; strong > *strongly*.
▶ Adjectives ending in -*ue* drop the -*e*: due > *duly*; true > *truly*.
▶ Adjectives ending in -*y* change to -*ily*: happy > *happily*;
  ready > *readily*; funny > *funnily*.
▶ Adjectives ending in -*ll* add -*y*: full > *fully*; shrill > *shrilly*.
▶ Adjectives ending in -*ic* usually add -*ally*: drastic > *drastically*;
  sarcastic > *sarcastically* (but note *publicly*).

Some adverbs have the same form as adjectives:

a *long* time (adjective), did you wait *long*? (adverb)
a *fast* horse (adjective), the car went *fast* (adverb)

Some adverbs affect the whole sentence, not just the verb:

> The book, *then*, makes an important contribution to our knowledge of food.

The adverb *then* has a dual purpose: it enlarges the meaning of the verb *makes*, and it also expresses a relationship between the whole sentence and what has gone before: in this case *then* expresses the conclusion. Other forms of relationships with what has gone before can also be expressed by adverbs, usually near the beginning of the sentence, e.g. *however, nevertheless, incidentally, moreover, likewise, besides, therefore.*

Prepositions

A preposition is a word that is placed before a noun or pronoun to link it to another part of the sentence or to the sentence as a whole. There are a large number of these, including: *at, in, to, by, from, with, through, round*:

> *On* the beach Rakdeep gazed *at* the dolphin *in* amazement.
> You must walk *round* the wood, not *through* it.
> Leon and Erica arrived *during* the afternoon, not *after* lunch as expected.

The preposition can affect the sense of some verbs, e.g. agree *with/on/to*:

> We agree *with* you and *with* the action you have taken.
> We agree *on* what we should do next.
> Your brother will not agree *to* our suggestion.

The same word may be a preposition or an adverb:

> Wait *outside* the door. (preposition)
> Wait *outside*. (adverb)

Many sentences naturally end with a preposition:

> What a mess your bedroom is *in*!
> The husband was easy to talk *to*; the wife impossible to
>   communicate *with*.
> What did you mend it *with*? Where is she *from*?

Nowadays this is acceptable, although in the past it was absolutely forbidden and writers used to go to great lengths to avoid it. The so-called rule was famously ridiculed by Sir Winston Churchill (1874–1965) when he referred to 'the sort of English up with which I will not put' when more naturally he could have spoken of 'the sort of English I will not put up with'.

On the other hand, a preposition at the end of a clause or sentence can sometimes sound awkward, especially in a more formal context:

> This is the college I spent three happy years *at*.

This would be better reworded:

> This is the college *at which* I spent three happy years.

Conjunctions

A conjunction connects two words or groups of words:

> blue *and* white stripes; take it *or* leave it;
> I went to bed early *because* I was tired.

It need not always be placed between the words being linked:

> *Because* I was tired, I went to bed early.
> *Although* he was injured, he went on playing.

It is possible for a word to be a conjunction in one sentence and
have a different function in another:

> Look *before* you leap. (conjunction)
> It has happened *before*. (adverb)
> We left *before* the end. (preposition)

Interjections or exclamations

An interjection or exclamation is a word or remark expressing
emotion, usually sudden:

> *Aha*! So it was you! You didn't expect to be caught, *eh*?
> *Ouch*! That hurt!
> *Alas*, it was the dog that died!

Words with more than one function

English grammar is very flexible and there are many examples of words performing several functions. For example, the nouns *dog*, *bus*, *leg* and *school* can all be used as verbs:

> I'm going to *leg* it home.
> It is sensible to *bus* the children to school.

The word *down* is a good example of a multi-function word:

> Put it *down*! (adverb)
> Let's walk *down* the hill. (preposition)
> The pillows are filled with *down*. (noun)
> A *down* payment of £10. (adjective)
> The workforce decided to *down* tools. (verb)

10 THINGS TO REMEMBER

1 *Parts of speech (or word classes) define the functions of words.*

2 *The essentials of communication are noun and verb: an object, person or quality and what he, she, or it does or is. Other parts of speech are defined by the roles they play in linking together these basic parts of speech.*

3 *Three other parts of speech can be defined by their relationship with nouns or verbs: for example, a pronoun stands in place of a noun.*

4 *Adverbs and adjectives tell us more about verbs and nouns; it is obvious from the names which one tells us about which.*

5 *Words are defined by function, so that is a pronoun when it stands alone, an adjective when it supports a noun.*

6 *A preposition (from the Latin 'place before') goes in front of a noun to link it to the rest of the sentence.*

7 *Conjunctions (from the Latin 'join together') join different parts of the sentence.*

8 *These words also define the relationship between the two words, phrases or clauses being linked. A simple example of this is found in words such as* after *and* before, *which are both conjunctions and prepositions.*

9 *There are many examples of words operating as more than one part of speech.*

10 *In many such cases the meaning is the same, while the function changes. For instance,* attack *as noun and verb has the same meaning. However, the same word can come from a totally different source. For instance,* down *generally has the same basic meaning, even as a verb (to* down *an opponent or a drink), but then we also find it as a noun meaning a gently rolling hill or soft feathers.*

3

....

Sentence structure

In this chapter you will learn about:
- *the basic units of language: subject, object, complement, verbs and tenses, phrases and clauses.*

Basic units of language

A sentence communicates a complete action, thought or feeling to the reader or listener:

> Don kicked the ball.
> Michael thought she was in the kitchen.
> You should consider the matter most carefully.
> We were sorry you couldn't come to the party.

It may contain a maximum of five elements:

> subject; verb; object(s); complement; adverbial.

but the shortest possible complete sentence need only consist of noun or pronoun (subject) and verb:

> Ted ran. He ran.
> Sue was singing. We were sorry.

In what appear to be incomplete sentences, the noun may be implied, not stated, or it may refer to words that went before:

> Run!
> Keep off the grass.
> Don. (in answer to 'Who kicked the ball?')
> Yes. (in answer to previous question)

Insight

In conversation or in a written piece that simulates conversation a sentence may be given in an incomplete form: 'But who is responsible for this state of affairs? The Government.' This is obviously short for, 'The Government is responsible for this state of affairs.' However, there is one form of sentence which – in full – can dispense with a subject: the imperative or command. If you are telling somebody to do something, clearly the subject of the verb is implied as the person spoken to. In old-fashioned sentence analysis, pupils some 50 years ago would write '(You)' as the subject of the sentence, 'Run!'.

Subject

The person or thing that performs the action of the verb is known as the subject of the sentence – when in doubt ask the question *Who* or *What did this*?

The subject may be a noun, a pronoun, or a set of words:

> *She* did a cartwheel but *he* fell over.
> *The cars* were lined up on the grid.

Sometimes the subject of the sentence is a form of the verb such as a verbal noun (noun formed from a verb ending in *-ing*), as in:

> *Swimming* would be foolhardy.
> *Shopping* is easier on Mondays.

or a group of words (phrase) beginning with the *to* form of the verb (known as the infinitive) such as:

To delay too long would be risky.

Object

The object of the verb is the person or thing that receives the action of the verb. It may be a noun, a pronoun, or a set of words. It is not essential for a verb to have an object. Some verbs never take an object (e.g. *sleep*, *rise*): these are called **intransitive** verbs.

She was sleeping. They are trying very hard.

If a verb has an object it is called a **transitive** verb:

I stubbed *my toe*. Do you like *the colour*? Try *jogging*.

Some verbs sometimes have an object:

The neighbours *were burning* garden rubbish.

and at other times do not have an object:

The lamps *were burning* brightly.

There are two kinds of object:

Direct object – a word or set of words affected directly by the verb:

They welcomed *him*.
She asked *what we were doing*.

Indirect object – a word or set of words *to* or *for* which the action of the verb is performed.

The shop sold *him* a faulty camera.
They sent an offer of a refund to *all their customers*.

> ## Insight
> How do you tell an indirect object from a direct object? It
> can be a matter of word order, the indirect coming before the
> direct: 'The committee awarded the theatre group the prize.'
> If, however, you wish to alter that word order, you must add
> 'to' in front of the indirect object: 'The committee awarded
> the prize to the theatre group.'

Complement

Instead of or as well as an object, some verbs are followed by what
is called a **complement** to complete the sentence. This may refer to
the subject or the object:

SUBJECT COMPLEMENTS

Some verbs (e.g. to *become, taste, seem, appear, look*) express a
state rather than an action, and the rest of the sentence refers back
to the subject of the verb:

> The cat looked *ill*.
> The atmosphere *remained tense*.

Note the difference between:

> He *made* a rice pudding

and

> He *made* an excellent goalkeeper.

OBJECT COMPLEMENTS

Some verbs are followed by a word or group of words that complete the meaning of the verb by referring to its object:

> They kept it *secret*.
> I thought them a *bit rude*.

Agreement of subject and verb

When the subject is singular the verb must be singular to 'agree' with it:

> Sandra *is* at home and so *is* her sister.
> She *hears* her brother shouting and *wonders* why.
> The dog *was* lying on the ground on its side.

When the subject is plural, the verb must be plural too:

> Sandra and her sister *are* at home.
> They *hear* their brothers shouting and *wonder* why.

Take care, when using longer sentences which contain two or more clauses, to make the verb agree with its own subject:

> The dog *sees* the rabbits which *are* quietly feeding and *runs* towards them.
> Joe, whose friends *are* all staring at him, quickly *leaves* the room.

Insight

The question of subject–verb agreement can be tricky. When there are several elements involved, there's a temptation to use the plural, but that is not always correct. 'The assessment

(Contd)

of the difficulties of managing the transfer ...' is singular: there are many difficulties, but only one assessment. 'The team of 15 archaeologists ...' is singular because there is only one team. 'The mayor, with many visiting dignitaries ...' is singular because 'the mayor' is the subject; 'The mayor and visiting dignitaries' would be plural.

Verbs and tenses

The tense of a verb is the form it takes to make it clear when an action takes place or a state existed. We can describe an event as taking place in the past, or as happening in the present while we write, or as occurring at some time in the future.

The verbs we use to tell of these events must be in the corresponding tense: past, present or future.

Past tenses	Present tenses	Future tenses
He kicked the ball	He kicks the ball	He will kick the ball
He has kicked the ball	He is kicking the ball	He will be kicking the ball
He has been kicking the ball	He does kick the ball	He will have been kicking the ball
He was kicking the ball	The ball is being kicked	He will have kicked the ball
He did kick the ball		
The ball was being kicked		
He had kicked the ball		
He had been kicking the ball		

In writing, the simple rule is to keep to the tense you begin with unless there is some good reason to change it. The verbs in the following passage are all in the same tense, describing a sequence of actions in the past:

> Jack shouted. The figure instantly disappeared. Jack moved cautiously forward. A cobweb brushed against his forehead, startling him.

In the following passage, look at the verbs in italics and work out why the tenses have been correctly changed.

> At six o'clock this evening, his wife will be going to him. By then *he will have been working* for 56 hours non-stop. If his calculations *are* correct, it *was* the chemical he *told* us about that caused the explosion. As she *goes* to take him home, I *shall be* waiting outside.

FINITE AND NON-FINITE VERB FORMS

The form of the verb that has a subject and a tense is called **finite**:

> Everyone *uses* computers.
> He *surfed* the net. They *ate* a pizza.

A verb is in a **non-finite** form when it does not have a subject or does not form a whole tense, in which case it is either an **infinitive** form or a form of **participle**:

Infinitive

> It's easy *to understand*.
> *To surf* the net you need *to get* online.

The infinitive need not be a 'to' form. If it follows a verb such as *can, could, would, should, must, may, might, shall* or *will*, 'to' is not present:

> We might *eat* a pizza this evening.
> You must *get up* early tomorrow.

Participle

Participles are of two kinds:

▶ '-ing' words, such as *running*, *walking*, *shopping*, which may
appear with different functions in the sentence:

Running is good exercise. (verbal noun)
People were *running* from the building. (part of a tense)
They fought a *running* battle. (adjective)

▶ '-ed' forms (or -d, -t, -en, -n, etc. See list of irregular verbs
on pages 206–210). The '-ed' form is a verb form that is
sometimes part of a tense:

He has *complained*. I had not *kept* fit.
Have you *chosen*?

or it may be used as an adjective:

bruised feelings, *burnt* toast, *sworn* enemies, etc.

ACTIVE AND PASSIVE VERBS

A verb is active when the subject of the sentence performs the
action:

I *misled* you.
The company *built* the stadium.
The crew *launched* the life-boat.

It is passive when the subject of the sentence is the object of the
action, or, in other words, 'suffers' the action:

I was *misled* by you.
The stadium was *built* by the company.
The life-boat was *launched* by the crew.

Phrases

A phrase is a set of words containing a single idea that does not contain a finite verb. It has the same function in a sentence as a noun or pronoun, adjective or adverb.

	Type of phrase
His *former friends* helped him. Do you know *his time of arrival*?	noun
None of the students failed.	pronoun
The paper will not be published *because of the strike*. Ring me *before the end of the morning*.	adverbial

Sir James, *arrogant as ever*, emerged
   from his Daimler.
The tower, *now fallen into disrepair*, was
   demolished.
	adjectival

A phrase may contain a non-finite '-*ing*' or '*to*' form of the verb:

> *Walking fast* is an excellent exercise.
> The people *hurrying from the field* were panic-stricken.
> I heard his radio *playing loud music*.
> We decided *to run round the garden*.

It may be used with an *-ed* form as in:

He woke up *refreshed by his sleep.*

Clauses

A clause is a set of words that contains a finite verb. If it makes sense on its own it is called a main clause: *He was angry* and *he slammed the door.*

If a clause does not make sense on its own it is called a subordinate clause. Like phrases, subordinate clauses perform different functions in the sentence:

	Type of clause
What he said surprised everyone.	noun – subject
She regretted *that she had lost her temper.*	noun – object
The tower, *which was falling down*, has been demolished.	adjectival
The Prime Minister, *who was in France*, made a speech.	adjectival
I was only nine *when my parents divorced.*	adverbial – when
I haven't a clue *where I have put it.*	adverbial – where
He slammed the door *because he was angry.*	adverbial – why
They played *as they had never played before.*	adverbial – how

10 THINGS TO REMEMBER

1 *A sentence can be as little as two words – a subject and an intransitive verb: 'Mary won.'*

2 *On the other hand a complex sentence can contain several main and subordinate clauses: 'When she recovered from her exertions in the semi-final, which had been very tiring, Mary played her best tennis and, even though her opponent was a former champion, Mary won the championship when she served brilliantly in the second set.'*

3 *As the above examples show, there are some verbs (in this case won) which can be used both transitively and intransitively.*

4 *In conversation or in newspaper headlines, a sort of shorthand can be used to create non-sentences where the full structure is implied: 'Four cups of coffee, please' or 'Two dead in motorway pile-up'.*

5 *All full sentences have a subject, except for commands, where the subject is implied.*

6 *A finite verb is the most essential element of a sentence. A non-finite verb does not indicate time and cannot take a subject.*

7 *Direct and indirect objects can exist side by side; direct objects can be used on their own ('He drives a car').*

8 *Complements can take many forms. It is a good idea to remember the meaning of the word (something that completes). If there is no object, but the sentence needs something to complete the meaning, that is the complement. In 'He found the camp in the woods', 'in the woods' is not the complement because 'He found the camp' makes sense, but in 'The camp is*

(Contd)

in the woods', 'in the woods' is the complement because it is necessary to complete the meaning.

9 *A sentence with a passive verb does not always indicate who did the action.*

10 *A clause differs from a phrase in that it contains a finite verb.*

4

Punctuation (1)

In this chapter you will learn:
- *about the full stop, question mark, exclamation mark, comma, hyphen and apostrophe*
- *about capital letters*.

When we speak, we use various speech patterns to make our meaning clear to the listener. We raise and lower our voices, pause for longer or shorter intervals, speak more quickly or more slowly, more loudly or more softly, and emphasize certain words and not others. We also help to make our meaning clear with body language – facial expressions, gestures and body movements.

However, when we write, we have only a set of punctuation marks to represent these speech patterns and body language. Used correctly, these rules make the meaning of what we write clear to the reader.

Full stop (.)

The full stop is used to end a sentence and so separates one sentence from another.

> Wayne is a fine cricketer. He often scores half a century in our league matches. He is also a very good fast bowler.

Listen. You cannot go yet. You must stay here until they tell you you can leave.

It is also used in incomplete sentences such as:

Fine, thank you. (answer to a query about someone's health)
No, certainly not. (answer to the question 'Will you do it?')

Its second important use is to mark certain abbreviated words:

i.e. (Latin *id est* = that is, followed by an explanation of what has gone before)
e.g. (Latin *exempli gratia* = for example)
etc. (Latin *et cetera* = and so on, and the others)

but it is no longer necessary in NB (Latin *nota bene*) or PS (*post scriptum*).

It is used in some abbreviated titles:

Prof. A.R. Taylor

It is not normally the practice to use a full point if the last letter of the abbreviation is the same as the last letter of the full form of the word:

Mr, Mrs, Ms, Dr, St (street and saint), Rd, 4th, etc.

nor is it necessary to use it with academic degrees such as MA or BSc or with honours such as KCB, DSO, or other titles such as MP.

It is optional to use full points in:

a.m. and p.m. (Latin *ante* and *post meridiem*)
A.D. (*anno domini*) and B.C. (before Christ)
R.S.V.P. (*répondez s'il vous plaît* = please reply).

Most names made from initial letters such as BBC, ITV, EU and NATO are spelt without full stops.

The full point is needed as a decimal point in units of money (£20.40) and percentages (19.5 per cent), and is found in expressions of time to separate hours from minutes (13.25).

Question mark (?)

The question mark is needed at the end of a sentence that poses a question:

Who was that on the telephone?

even though a question may be worded as a statement:

You don't really believe that?

explanation justifies it. It is certainly correct to state that 'You don't really believe that?' needs a question mark, but to say that a question mark should follow a question worded as a statement is – shall we say? – questionable.

A question mark is also needed at the end of a quoted question:

'Who was that on the telephone?' she asked.

At the end of a sentence, the question mark has the force of a full stop and is followed by a capital letter. Do not use a question mark *and* a full stop.

A question mark is not used at the end of a reported or implied (as distinct from a direct) question:

She asked who was on the telephone.
I'd like to know whether or not you'll be coming.

Exclamation mark (!)

The exclamation mark is used instead of a full stop at the end of a sentence expressing strong feelings, such as surprise, anger or enthusiasm.

Put that down at once!
What a splendid idea!

It allows the writer to choose between a mild expression of feeling:

I never dreamt he would be so stupid. Please listen.

and a stronger one:

I never dreamt he would be so stupid! Please listen!

You also use it after single words or phrases (greeting, expletives, toasts, warnings, commands, cries for help, insults, etc.) which have an exclamatory nature:

Ow! Good heavens! You idiot! Look out! What a pity!
Hello! Hi! Cheers! Help! Hey!

It is not a rule that such expressions have to be followed by an exclamation mark; you have to decide whether the context calls for special strength. Note the difference between

Hello there! Can you hear me?
Good heavens! That's incredible!

and

Hello, how are you?
Good heavens. That was ages ago.

Comma (,)

The comma separates words, phrases or clauses when the sense demands a slight pause. There are few rules for it: its use is often a matter of taste or emphasis. The most common error, apart from using a comma when a full stop is essential, is over-use in a way that interrupts the flow of a sentence.

The best policy is to use a comma only when it contributes something to the sense.

ITEMS IN LISTS

Commas are needed in lists of nouns, adjectives, verbs or adverbs:

Butter, milk, eggs and cheese are in short supply.
The play was long, boring, tasteless, and badly acted.

The children laughed, cheered and shouted.
It should be sung softly, gently and lightly.

A comma before *and* introducing the final item in a list is optional but normally unnecessary. There is no need for commas when a list of adjectives precedes a noun in a flowing way:

A big old orange estate car drew up alongside.

but commas help emphasis if adjectives jar with each other:

An angular, twitching, untidy-looking young man.

The comma is also used in a list of phrases or clauses (main or subordinate):

His favourite relaxations are listening to music, cultivating raspberries, and sailing his boat at weekends. *(phrases)*

We went to a restaurant, spent a long time over our meal, and talked of old times. *(main clauses)*

He said that he had bought the house as a ruin, renovated it at considerable expense, and then sold it. *(subordinate clauses)*

In such longer constructions, a comma before *and* introducing the final item is a helpful signpost, but it is not obligatory, and some people would argue that it is superfluous and fussy.

Insight

The purpose of all punctuation is to make meaning clearer, and this is especially true of the comma, which has a sort of roving commission to indicate small pauses when needed. Lists are punctuated by commas, but what if the elements in the list are long and have commas within them? The solution can be to use semicolons, not because of any rule, but simply to help the reader: 'The Library committee decided to order the complete works of Francis Brett Young, a local author of considerable eminence; up-to-date versions of several major dictionaries, including a dictionary of American English; further copies of Alan Bennett's *Untold Stories*, which has proved astonishingly popular; and several volumes of political memoirs.' (The third semicolon, just like the final comma in any list, is optional.)

MARKING OFF CLAUSES

Use a pair of commas to separate information inserted into a sentence which therefore interrupts the sense. Don't forget the second of the pair:

> When the battle ceased after four long months, and after the gains and losses had been painfully reckoned, the bitter truth at last became apparent.

> The animal, which until then had been sleeping, suddenly leapt to its feet.

> Having managed to climb the ladder, though it had creaked ominously from time to time, he began to feel less apprehensive.

The comma is not always needed to mark off a clause or phrase; its assistance is seldom required in a simple construction.

> When you come back it will be finished.
> In all the excitement he had not noticed the time.

Even so, the lack of a comma in even a short sentence may cause momentary ambiguity or untidiness. In:

> From the hill beyond the village looks smaller.

the reader gets as far as *looks* before realizing that village is the subject of the verb, not the object of *beyond*. A comma after beyond makes the structure clear.

MARKING WORDS IN APPOSITION

Add a pair of commas to mark off words in apposition:

> The writer, a man deeply interested in the sense of community, described the suburbs as being peopled by rootless beings, nomads who have no tribe.

MARKING PARENTHESES

Insert commas to mark off words which are not part of the central structure of a sentence but inserted by way of parenthesis. These include:

▸ additions such as *I think*, *in conclusion*, *of course*, *yes*, *no*, *isn't it*, *please*, *thank you*;
▸ the names of persons being addressed;
▸ exclamations that are part of a sentence;
▸ linking adverbs (e.g. *however*, *moreover*, *therefore*, *perhaps*, *nevertheless*) and corresponding phrases (e.g. *on the other hand*, *on the whole*, *even so*) which relate a sentence to a preceding one.

In all cases, commas should be used only when the sense of parenthesis is present.

Commas should not be used between subject and verb or to link two sentences, however short:

> Please come soon, I miss you.
> A meeting has been arranged, this will be held next week.

In the first of these a colon or a dash should replace the comma, because the second statement explains the first. In the second you could use a semicolon or a comma plus 'and', to indicate a relationship between the two statements. Alternatively, a full stop followed by a capital letter would be possible in both examples.

MOST COMMON MISTAKE

As several of the above explanations show, commas are often used in pairs to mark off parts of sentences. A common mistake is to forget the second comma:

> Famine, as has often been noticed is prevalent in ...
> Drama classes, despite their popularity with younger members have had to be withdrawn.

Punctuation is needed after *noticed* and *members* to complete the parenthesis.

Hyphen (1)

Hyphens are normally used after such prefixes as *vice* (vice-captain), *ex* (ex-serviceman), *self* (self-conscious) and *non* (non-starter), and are usually needed before *up* (close-up) and *off* (brush-off) in the formation of compound words. Thus

> She gave him the brush-off.

but

> Brush off the cobwebs.

Hyphens are always needed between a prefix and a proper noun:

> pro-American, un-English, ex-President.

Compound adjectives are often made by combining adjectives and nouns:

> *middle-class* values, *full-time* job, *west-country* town, *short-term* prospects, *left-wing* views.

The hyphen is not used when such words are used as straightforward adjectives and nouns, not as compounds:

> a town in the west country, the left wing of the party.

In the same way, hyphens found in other compounds (*out-of-date equipment*) should be dropped when the same words are used with their normal grammatical function (The equipment is *out of date*).

Hyphens should always be used in words which, unhyphenated, would be ambiguous (*re-form, re-sign, re-cover*) or ugly (*full-length, semi-invalid*).

You can use more than one hyphen in the interests of clarity. A *semi-house trained dog* implies that there exists a trained dog capable of being described as *semi-house*. The correct punctuation is *semi-house-trained dog*.

Insight

Hyphens indicate which words connect directly with each other. A good example is 'a fine-tooth (or fine-toothed) comb'. This is often pronounced as 'a fine tooth-comb', an error that can arise because this is something of a dead metaphor, but what could a tooth-comb be? The correct use of the hyphen tells us that we are talking about a comb (for hair, not teeth!) that has so little space between its teeth that (metaphorically) it's perfect for a detailed search.

Apostrophe

The apostrophe has two important functions: to indicate possession and to mark the place where something has been left out of a shortened word.

POSSESSION

Possession is denoted by adding an apostrophe followed by *s* to the end of a singular word:

> the family's plans, the firm's address, the orchestra's reputation

and an apostrophe without s to the end of a plural word ending in -*s*:

> ladies' shoes (i.e. shoes for *ladies*), the brothers' disagreement (i.e. the disagreement of the *brothers*).

This rule does not apply when a plural word does not end in -*s* (e.g. *men, children, women*). In such cases, the apostrophe followed by s is needed to denote possession:

> men's pyjamas, children's toys, women's magazines.

There is some disagreement about singular words ending in -*s*. Both *James' wife* and *James's wife* are acceptable. The former is perfectly clear; the latter reflects normal pronunciation more accurately. The modern preference for simplicity in punctuation favours the former:

> Keats' poetry, Guy Fawkes' night.

An apostrophe is never used with possessive pronouns:

> hers, yours, theirs, his, ours, whose, its

(when *its* = belonging to it: see below for *it's*). The possessive *one's* needs an apostrophe; the plural *ones*, of course, does not:

> One must do one's best.
> Those are the ones I like.

The apostrophe should be used in:

> a month's holiday, in a week's time, several years' imprisonment, a term's work, four hours' delay

and in:

> I must go to the butcher's. Their prices were lower than other companies'. (Here *butcher's* is short for *butcher's shop* and *companies'* is short for *companies' prices*.)

The apostrophe is often omitted in the names of well-known firms:

> *Barclays Bank.*

It is permissible, and increasingly common, not to use an apostrophe after a plural noun that has an adjectival rather than a possessive sense:

> accounts section, students union, social services department, girls school.

This is no excuse for omitting the apostrophe in a word which ends in -s specifically to indicate the possessive, not the plural: *men's club*, *Women's Institute* and *children's home* need apostrophes.

SHORTENED WORDS

Words are sometimes shortened to reflect the way they are commonly pronounced. The omitted letters are replaced by an apostrophe that marks the place in a word where something has been left out. Here are some examples:

> I am > *I'm*, it is > *it's*, you are > *you're*; we are > *we're*; they have > *they've*
> do not > *don't*; shall not > *shan't*; would not > *wouldn't*; she will > *she'll*
> cannot > *can't*; does not > *doesn't*; will not > *won't*; is not > *isn't*
> of the clock > *o'clock*; there is > *there's*; the summer of 1999 > the summer of *'99*.

Although short forms are general in speech and informal writing, be careful how you use them when writing more formally. Some of them, e.g. *I'm*, *it's*, are very common; others are less acceptable.

MOST COMMON MISTAKE

It is very common to put an apostrophe in words where there should not be one. As we have seen above, the words *yours*, *ours*, *theirs*, etc. never have an apostrophe. In addition, it is quite common to see it inserted in a normal plural word that never needs one (*cabbage's*, *tomatoe's*, *potato's*). This misuse has been aptly named the greengrocer's apostrophe!

Capital letters

Capital letters are needed at the beginnings of sentences, and in direct speech (see page 60). They are also used at the beginning of proper nouns and titles.

PROPER NOUNS

Nouns naming particular people (*The Queen of Spain*) and groups of people (the *French*), places (the *Lake District*), rivers (the *Thames*), buildings (*Manchester Town Hall*), institutions (the *Catholic Church*), establishments (*Guys Hospital*), firms (*British Telecom*), organizations (the *National Trust*), festivals (*Easter*, *Diwali*), castles, countries, towns, streets, months of the year, days of the week, mountains, pets, house names, etc. start with capital letters, as do adjectives formed from proper nouns (*French*, *Shakespearean*).

TITLES

The titles of books, films, plays, television programmes, newspapers, magazines, songs, etc., start with capital letters The first word of a title always has a capital; unimportant words in the title (*of*, *the*, *in*, *and*) are generally spelt without one (*Who wants to be a Millionaire?*, *Lord of the Flies*). The titles of people start with capital letters (*Dame Judi Dench*, the *Lord Chancellor*).

It is normal practice to use capital letters for the particular, and small letters for the general:

the Queen of England	but	the kings and queens of England
the Bishop of Birmingham	but	He was made a bishop
South Africa	but	We drove south
Edinburgh University	but	He had a university education
the Government	but	governments since 1945

Have fun with language!

1 *Rewrite these sentences, inserting the necessary punctuation marks:*

   a *My shopping list includes eggs butter bread marmalade jam tea coffee beans streaky bacon new potatoes a sizeable cauliflower and some leeks have I missed anything out*

   b *You can buy all these at sainsburys marks & spencer tesco or asda*

   c *the dresses were delightful shades of yellow orange green blue violet grey and beige*

2 *Rewrite these, inserting the necessary punctuation marks to make the sense absolutely clear:*

   a *nevertheless they said they would do it but they did not like the idea*

   b *as if to make doubly sure she repeated what she had just said although it was quite obvious her audience had heard every word to end with he sang the chorus again and we all joined in*

   c *the bull trotting towards us we began to run though poor Beth could only hobble*

10 THINGS TO REMEMBER

1 A terminal mark is required at the end of every sentence: full stop, question mark or exclamation mark.

2 An exclamation mark follows an exclamatory phrase which may not be a sentence ('Heavens above!'), but can also indicate the way in which any sentence is to be read or spoken.

3 A comma is an excellent servant, available to do many jobs, but it is not suitable for separating clauses without the help of a conjunction.

4 A hyphen is not a dash, though they look similar. A dash is an informal division in a sentence.

5 A hyphen joins together two or more words as one.

6 The apostrophe has two distinct purposes: to indicate possession and the omission of letters.

7 The apostrophe is followed by 's' when indicating possession. The 's' is omitted with plurals ending in '-s' ('both schools' results'), but not with plurals ending in a different letter ('both women's husbands').

8 The apostrophe indicating omission is placed where the letter(s) is (are) left out, not between words: 'don't', not 'do'nt'.

9 Use initial capital letters for all proper nouns.

10 When a name consists of more than one word, only capitalize the important words: News of the World.

5

Punctuation (2)

In this chapter you will learn:
- *about the colon, semicolon, hyphen, dashes, paired brackets and quotation marks.*

In Chapter 4 we looked at the uses of the basic punctuation marks – full stops, questions marks, exclamation marks, commas, capital letters and apostrophes. These basic tools enable us to write and punctuate most simple sentences. This chapter concentrates on some other, subtler ones – colons and semicolons, hyphens, dashes, paired brackets and quotation marks – which enable us to add more variety and emphasis, and finer nuances of meaning, to what we say.

Colon (:)

The colon is a sharp punctuation mark, second only to the full stop in weight. It often carries the general sense of 'that is to say', and has a number of uses.

INTRODUCING A LIST

Use a colon to introduce a list when the sense demands a pause:

> The car has a number of optional extras: sun roof, tinted windows, rear seat-belts, and electrically adjustable wing mirrors.

ANTICIPATING AN EXPLANATION

Use a colon to point forward to an explanation or an example:

> Choosing the kit was easy: there were three good sports shops within walking distance.
> There were far too many people present: long queues developed outside every tent.

LEADING UP TO A CLIMAX

Use a colon before a word or words which have a sense of climax or need emphasis:

> There can be only one reason for this delay: incompetence.
> At last he made up his mind: he would sell it.

Heavier emphasis could be given to *he would sell it* by putting a full stop and capital letter after mind. To do the same after *delay* in the first example is also permissible, but the resultant one-word 'sentence' *Incompetence*, may be over-dramatic.

MAKING A DRAMATIC BREAK

Use a colon rather than a comma when you want to make a sharper, more dramatic break between the introduction and the quotation or title:

> The quotation begins: 'All the world's a stage ...'.
> Consult page 12: 'Common faults'.

The colon does not need a following dash (:-). It is sufficient on its own.

Semicolon (;)

The semicolon is stronger than the comma and weaker than the full stop in the length of pause or degree of separation it imposes. It too has a number of uses.

JOINING TWO SENTENCES

Use a semicolon when you wish to join two sentences, especially short ones, to make a longer statement. It is especially useful when there is an element of comparison:

> The men are being noisy; the women are mostly silent.
> The earliest recorded events took place five hundred years ago; the latest were observed only last year.

BEFORE SOME LINKING WORDS

Use a semicolon rather than a comma before such linking words as *besides, however, nevertheless, as a result, for example, as a consequence, in any case, still*:

> I judged it to be too much trouble; however, the other members of the family disagreed.
> We knew it was a foolish thing to do; nevertheless, we tried.

Insight

The colon and the semicolon look very similar and it is possible to imagine situations where either would be acceptable. However, there is one big difference between them: the uses of the colon are precise and clearly laid out, the semicolon can be used widely or not at all. In most cases (including the example of 'Before some linking words') a full stop is also acceptable; in the case of the lists a comma is

(Contd)

technically the correct punctuation, though very confusing.
Using the semicolon skilfully is a mark of a flexible, even
elegant style.

SEPARATING ITEMS IN A LIST

Use the semicolon to separate items in a list when there are
commas within one or more of the items:

> The room contained two large bookcases, both made of wood,
> the books crammed in very tightly; a settee, the flowered
> material covering it very worn; four easy chairs, each of a
> different colour and shape.

> Many activities are planned: a party for the children, especially
> from single-parent families; a charity ball, the good cause to be
> advertised at a later date; a sports day, including events for
> the physically handicapped.

Hyphen (2)

The hyphen joins two or three words into a single entity:

> brother-in-law, bullet-proof, hair-raising, so-called,
> get-together.

It helps to prevent ambiguity or momentary confusion, as may be
seen by observing the differences between the following:

a geriatric ward nurse	*and*	a geriatric-ward nurse
extra marital sex	*and*	extra-marital sex
four wheeled vehicles	*and*	four-wheeled vehicles
forty odd customers	*and*	forty-odd customers
a little used car	*and*	a little-used car
main road traffic	*and*	main-road traffic

To lay down other rules for using hyphens is not easy because many hyphenated words (especially those with prefixes such as *post-*, *anti-*, *re-*, *pre-*, *by-*) gradually shed their hyphens as time goes by and begin to appear in dictionaries as single words. In recent years this has happened to *bypass*, *multinational*, *antifreeze* and *prenatal*, for example, though not all dictionaries agree.

IN NUMBERS AND FRACTIONS

Hyphens are used when writing out fractions (*four-fifths*), numbers between twenty-one and ninety-nine, and compound adjectives containing numbers or adjectives formed from numbers:

> four-storey building, eight-month delay, twelve-year-old boy, second-class citizens, three-and-a-half-hour meeting, first-floor bedroom, five-ton lorry.

Hyphens are not used in:

> a building of four storeys, a delay of eight months, a boy twelve years old, citizens who are second class, a meeting lasting three and a half hours, a bedroom on the first floor, a lorry weighing five tons

where no compound term is used.

IN COMPOUND ADJECTIVES

Many hyphenated expressions are compound adjectives consisting of a participle preceded by an adverb, adjective or noun:

> fast-moving, well-known, hard-earned, terror-stricken, medium-sized, blue-eyed, home-made, never-failing, hand-picked, wide-ranging, middle-aged, ill-tempered, best-selling, ready-made, long-winded.

The hyphen is not used in:

> The firm is well known/well equipped/well respected

because *known*, *equipped* and *respected* are part of the main verb, described by the adverb *well*, and not parts of compound adjectives.

> **Insight**
>
> Not all dictionaries agree on the need for hyphens in different compounds. There is often no logic in the decision. In simple terms there tends to be a progression over time from two words to hyphenated to one word, but this is very unpredictable. Try to explain *homeowner*, *home-grown* and *home help*. Ultimately this is not a priority: use common sense and a good dictionary (or this book) and don't worry about the odd mistake – everyone makes them, even dictionary compilers.

No hyphen is needed in the familiar adverb + adjective combination:

> an unusually fierce storm, a thoroughly mischievous suggestion.

Dashes

A single dash marks a sharp break in the sentence. The effect is more dramatic than using a semicolon or a colon:

> Occupation, influence, income, friends, wife – all were lost.
> I warned you – but you would not listen!
> She has made a close study of South Africa – its peoples, customs, languages, art and music.

It is also useful to introduce an afterthought, or sudden change of direction:

> That was the end of the matter – or so he thought.

And it can also be used when summing up:

> Courtesy, helpfulness, sympathy, good humour – these are
> among the most admired of attributes.

PAIRS OF DASHES

A pair of dashes can be used instead of a pair of commas when
inserting a parenthesis (an extra piece of information, often
resembling an afterthought) into a sentence:

> If she succeeds – and who dares say she will not? – she will
> have been the first in our family to do it.

Paired brackets

Brackets can be used to indicate parentheses. These have two main
purposes.

TO GIVE ADDITIONAL EXPLANATIONS

Here are some examples:

> The directions for assembling the model are very important
> (see pp. 7–11 of the instruction booklet).
> Sonic boom (shock waves of sound) may be compared to bow
> waves (shock waves of water) made by a vessel.

TO ENCLOSE ADDITIONAL INFORMATION

This has the effect of making the information less prominent, as
if hiding it away, than if a pair of commas or especially a pair of
dashes, had been used.

> The women (all except Nancy) began to cheer.
> The huge man (nearly seven feet tall, yellow teeth bared)
> raised his great fist menacingly.

Quotation marks

Quotation marks are also known as inverted commas or speech
marks. They are used to enclose types of material and can be used
in their single (') or double (") form.

Here are some of the types of material they can enclose:

DIRECT SPEECH

Here are some examples:

> Jasper said, 'I should like to go home now.'
> 'It is colder today than yesterday,' Mollie said.
> I said, 'Goodbye,' and he replied, 'See you again soon.'
> 'Jack!' shouted the teacher. 'Did you hear what I said?'
> This is exactly what she wrote: 'I never intend to write to you
> again as long as I live.'

TITLES OF SONGS, POEMS, PLAYS, ETC.

Use quotation marks for titles.

> The other evening we saw Shakespeare's 'The Tempest'.
> He has called his painting, 'Sunset on a Stormy Sea'.

Note that in print these would normally appear in italic, without quotation marks.

WORDS REFERRED TO AS WORDS

Use quotation marks when words are referred to as words rather than the things they stand for:

> The words 'sentence' and 'sincerely' are often misspelt.
> I said 'prohibited' not 'exhibited'.

Use double quotation marks for quotations within quotations if you are using single marks initially – and vice versa:

> She said, 'My boss is always saying, "Haven't you got any work to do?", then going away looking pleased with himself.'

CONVERSATIONS

Here are the rules for setting out and punctuating conversations:

▶ Begin a new paragraph when a person speaks, and also when you introduce sentences that come between one set of remarks and the next.
▶ Enclose between quotation marks the exact words spoken.
▶ Use a capital letter to begin the first word spoken.
▶ Use a comma to separate what comes before the words spoken from the words themselves. Alternatively, you can use a colon if you want to make a sharper break.
▶ When the last word spoken is the end of the statement, put the full stop *inside* the last quotation mark.
▶ When the words spoken form a question or an exclamation, put the question mark or exclamation mark inside the last quotation mark.
▶ When the words spoken do not form a complete sentence, put the comma *inside* the last quotation mark to separate it from what follows.

The passage below illustrates the rules you should follow when writing a dialogue between two or more people:

'Now pay attention, all of you,' Mrs Greenslade said.

All the pupils except Jack put their pens down and settled back in their seats sighing.

'Jack!' shouted the teacher. 'Did you hear me?'

Startled, Jack looked up. He hurriedly put down his pen and said, 'No, Miss, I didn't.'

Mrs Greenslade frowned at him and said, 'Then you must be deaf.'

Bob timidly raised his hand and waited.

'Well, Robert, what is it?'

Bob cleared his throat and said huskily, 'Please, Miss, can I go now?' He blinked nervously. 'My mum's got to go to the surgery at 12 o'clock, and I have to look after the baby.'

The class began to titter at the expression on the teacher's face as she glared at poor Bob.

10 THINGS TO REMEMBER

1 *Inserting a hyphen between two words can produce a meaning different from the two words separately ('a little used car' and 'a little-used car'), so it is worth taking care with your use of the hyphen.*

2 *On the other hand, it is sometimes difficult to see the reason for a word being hyphenated or not ('home-made' and 'home brew').*

3 *Adjectives tend to be hyphenated more than nouns, so you might find 'the home brew' but 'home-brewed beer', but here, as ever, clarity, not pedantry, is the main concern.*

4 *The colon has specific uses: introducing a list, an explanation, an amplification or a quotation.*

5 *A semicolon requires more finesse in its use: half-way between a full stop and a comma, it is useful for making a sharp break between things that you don't want to separate totally.*

6 *Parentheses are (as it were) inserts into the sentence. Commas can be used to mark them, but, if the parentheses are of any length, dashes or brackets are safer.*

7 *In a printed or word-processed text it is better to use italics for titles rather than quotation marks, which can be over-used.*

8 *In direct speech the quotation marks go round the exact words spoken – and no more.*

9 *In indirect or reported speech quotation marks are not used.*

10 *If the quoted speech contains a question or an exclamation, be careful to place the question or exclamation mark inside the quotation marks.*

6

Help with spelling

In this chapter you will learn:
- *the rules of spelling*
- *about the formation of plurals*
- *to recognize commonly misspelt words.*

It is often tempting, in these days of computer spellcheckers, to assume that being able to spell correctly is less important than other skills. Yet an ability to spell makes it much easier to write fluently, without constantly having to stop and check. You won't always have a computer or a dictionary to consult and, in any case, spellcheckers are not always reliable – they will not, for example, pick up on misspellings like those in *there house is over their; it was a pane the pain of glass was broken.*

The difficulty with so-called spelling rules in English is that the exceptions to any rule often outnumber the words that obey it. However, many groups of words do in fact follow certain patterns and it is these patterns which are set out below.

Doubling letters

Words with a single final consonant double before an ending beginning with a vowel (e.g. *-ing, -ed, -er, -able, -ous, -ible, -en*):

- ▶ if the word is one syllable with a short vowel:
  fat – fatten, fatter, fattest; fit – fitted, fitting, fitter
- ▶ if the word has more than one syllable and the stress is on the final syllable:
  begin – beginning, beginner; refer – referred, referral, referring

But note that there is no doubling of the single final consonant:

- ▶ if the word is one syllable with a long vowel or a double vowel:
  seat – seated, seating; look – looking, looked
- ▶ if the word has more than one syllable and the stress is before the final syllable:
  benefit – benefited; totter – tottering, tottered; focus – focused
  Exceptions: handicap – handicapped, handicapping; kidnap – kidnapper, etc.; worship – worshipped, etc.; travel – travelled, etc.

Words ending in -*w*, -*x*, -*y* or in double consonants never double the final letter.

Insight

The double forms of some of these words, e.g. *benefitted* and *focussed*, are generally judged to be acceptable alternatives these days. You must use your own judgement – or, if you prefer it, your own judgment.

Doubling the l

Words ending in a single -*l* preceded by a single vowel double the -*l* before an ending that starts with a vowel:

    cancel – cancelling, cancellation, cancelled
    control – controller, controlled, controlling
    Exception: parallel – paralleled

The -*l* is not doubled if it is not preceded by a single vowel:

> cool – cooler, cooled, cooling, coolest
> snarl – snarling, snarled
> Exceptions: wool – woollen; dial – dialled, dialling

The doubling rule does not apply before endings that start with a consonant:

> instal – installed, installation *but* instalment
> rival – rivalling, rivalled *but* rivalry

Double the -*l* if you want to add -*y*:

> loyal – loyally; normal – normally
> Exception: oil – oily

Thus adjectives ending -*ful* form adverbs ending -*fully*.

Insight

For many people -*ful* words present quite a problem. It is a natural reaction to spell them -*full* because the words mean full of something, but, if you're full of spite or help, you're *spiteful* or *helpful*. An allied word that causes widespread confusion is *fulfil*, with many gravitating to the American spelling *fulfill* – or even *fullfill* or *fullfil*, which are just wrong.

When to omit the final -e

A silent *e* at the end of a word is

▶ retained before an ending that starts with a consonant;
  definite – definitely; move – movement
  Exceptions: argue – argument; hate – hatred; true – truly;
  nine – ninth

▶ dropped before an ending that starts with a vowel:
become – becoming; fame – famous; value – valuable
Exceptions: mile – mileage; sale – saleable; rate – rateable

Words ending in -ye, -ee, -oe retain the final -e before the ending -ing:

eye – eyeing; agree – agreeing

With words ending -ce and -ge, the final -e is

▶ retained before an ending that starts with a consonant:
strange – strangely; discourage – discouragement
▶ retained before -ous and -able:
outrage – outrageous; service – serviceable
▶ dropped before other endings:
notice – noticing, noticed (but noticeable);
ice – icy, de-icer, icing, icily

---

ei or ie?

When the sound is ee: i comes before e, except after c:

achieve; believe; chief; field; fiend; hygiene; piece; relief;
 retrieve; shield
After c: ceiling; conceit; deceit; perceive; receipt; receive
Exceptions: seize, species

When the sound is ay: e comes before i:

eight; foreign; freight; neighbour; rein; reign; skein; sleight;
weight; veil; vein

When the sound is eye: e comes before i:

eiderdown; either; height; neither; kaleidoscope

Note: some *ie* and *ei* words are pronounced differently and have to be learnt individually: e.g. *friend*, *pierce*, *variety*; *weird*. Also, *either* and *neither* can be pronounced with *ee*.

Changing y to i

Words ending in *-y* preceded by a consonant change the *y* to *i* before all endings except *-ing*:

> easy – easier, easily, easiest; dry – drier, dries, dried but
> drying (exception: dryness); occupy – occupier, occupies,
> occupied *but* occupying; copy – copier, copies, copied *but*
> copying
> Exceptions: shy – shyness, shyly; sly – slyly

Words ending in *-y* preceded by a vowel retain the *y* before an ending:

> convey – conveyed, conveying, conveyance;
> delay – delaying, delayed
> Exceptions: pay – paying *but* paid; say – saying *but* said;
> gay – gaily

-ise or -ize?

The endings *-ise* and *-ize* are often interchangeable, likewise *-isation* and *-ization*. The *-ise* ending is usually safe (but note *prize*, meaning 'award'). If you want to use *-ize* remember that certain spellings are invariable (e.g. *compromise*, *revise*, *supervise*). American English favours *-ize*.

Miscellaneous

Nouns ending -*our* form adjectives ending -*orous*:

>   humour – humorous; vigour – vigorous

The letter *q* is always followed by *u* and a vowel, except in some words of foreign origin, e.g. *al-Qaida*.

Words ending -*ie* change the -*ie* to -*y* before -*ing*:

>   tie – tying (*but* tied); lie – lying; die – dying

The sound *seed* at the end of words is spelt -*sede* in only one case (*supersede*), -*ceed* in only three (*proceed*, *exceed*, *succeed*) and -*cede* in all other words.

Words ending in -*c* add -*k* before endings beginning with *e*, *i* or *y*:

>   panic – panicked, panicking, panicky

The formation of plurals

Most nouns form the plural by adding -*s*.

Nouns ending in -*s*, -*ss*, -*x*, -*z*, -*ch*, -*sh*, -*o* add -*es*:

>   bonuses, losses, boxes, matches, potatoes, dishes
>   Exceptions: photos, radios, kilos, twos, solos, zeros, studios,
>   dynamos

Nouns endings in a single -*f* or -*fe* change these endings to -*ves*:

>   half – halves; life – lives
>   Exceptions: chiefs, roofs, beliefs, proofs

Nouns ending in -*y* preceded by a consonant change -*y* into -*ies*:

> party – parties; factory – factories

If the *y* is preceded by a vowel, simply add *s*: day – days.

Some nouns of Latin origin ending -*is* change the -*is* to -*es*:

> basis – bases, axis – axes, emphasis – emphases, crisis – crises

Many words of foreign origin have irregular plurals:

> phenomenon – phenomena

If dictionaries offer a choice between a foreign plural and an English one (gymnasium – gymnasia, gymnasiums), choose the English one.

In hyphened compounds, only the appropriate noun takes the plural:

> brothers-in-law, passers-by

If there is no noun, add *s* at the end:

> lay-bys, go-betweens, stand-bys, take-offs

It is now normal to place *s* at the end of

> bucketfuls, pocketfuls, spoonfuls.

List of words commonly misspelt

....

absence	across	apparatus
abysmal	address	appearance
accessible	advertisement	argument
accidentally	allege	arrangement
accommodation	already	attach
acknowledge	although	awkward
acquaint	amount	
acquire	annual	

....

basically	beginning	benefited
beautiful	believe	business
because		

....

calendar	commitment	conscientious
catarrh	committed	conscious
choose/chose	committee	consensus
ceiling	comparative	consolidate
cellar	comparison	control
college	conscience	criticism

....

daily	desperately	disagreeable
debt	detached	disappear
deceit	develop	disappointed
defence	development	discipline
definite	different	dissatisfied
description	difference	
desirable	diminution	

....

eighth	excellent	existence
efficient	excessive	expense
embarrassment	excite, exciting	extraordinary
equipment	excitement	exuberant
exaggerate	exercise	
exceed	exhilarating	

familiar	fortunately	fulfil
favourite	fortieth	fulfilled
February	forty	

gauge	grammar	guarantee
glamorous	grateful	guard
government	grievous	

harass	heir	humorous
hare-brained	honorary	humour
height	holiday	

idiosyncrasy	incidentally	instalment
immediately	independence	interested
imminent	install	irrelevant

jewellery/jewelry

| knowledge | knack | knuckle |

| liaison | lieutenant | loose/lose |
| leisure | | |

maintain	medicine	miscellaneous
maintenance	miniature	mischievous
marvellous		

| necessarily | niece | noticeable |
| neighbour | ninth | nuisance |

occasion	occurred	omission
occasionally	occurrence	omit
occur	occurring	opportunity

paid	precede	proceed
panicked	preceding	profession
parallel(ed)	prefer(red)	prominent
parliament	prejudice	pseudonym

particularly	premises	publicly
pastime	preparation	pursue
playwright	privilege	pursuing
possess	procedure	

quay	queue	quiet/quite

receipt	refer(red)	relevant
receive	recognize	repetition
recommend		

schedule	siege	strength
scissors	sieve	succeed
seize	skilful	supersede
sentence	stationary	suppress
separate	stationery	surprise

temporary	tragedy	twelfth
tendency	truly	tie, tied, tying

undoubtedly	unnecessary	until
unmistakable	unparalleled	

vicious	vigorous	vinegar

waist	Wednesday	wilful
waste	weird	woollen

10 THINGS TO REMEMBER

1 *Rules in English always have exceptions, but it is not right to claim there are no rules. It is worth learning the rules as, though not infallible, they will decrease the percentage of error.*

2 *The old faithful 'i before e except after c' is one of the most helpful, but you must add 'when the sound is ee'.*

3 *Variation in pronunciation can cause a problem here. No one wishes to change the pronunciation of those who say 'eether', as in the song, but for spelling purposes they must accept that those who say 'eyether' are correct.*

4 *The endings -ise and -ize are often interchangeable, likewise -isation and -ization. The -ise ending is usually safe in British English. American English favours -ize.*

5 *A strangely common error is to regard* phenomena *as singular – also* criteria. *They are taken from Greek and are the plurals of* phenomenon *and* criterion.

6 *Most foreign borrowings have English plurals, at least as an alternative, but there is a considerable group of Latin nouns ending in -is that form plurals with -es. A variation is* appendix/appendices, *though* appendixes *is now acceptable.*

7 *Words that end in -our often discard the u when forming adjectives. However, the rule is not simple:* honour *gives us* honourable *and* honorary.

8 *It is sometimes necessary to shake off too close a relationship with the root words.* Maintain *seems certain to give us* maintainance, *but the correct noun is* maintenance.

9 *On the other hand awareness of the original words helps us to place the double consonants in the right place in* disappoint *and* disappear.

10 *A word not in the original list,* (in)convenient(ce) *has been a growth area for error. It's essential to keep the ie in its place; otherwise many variants on* inconvient *appear.*

7

Words that get confused

In this chapter you will learn:
- *about words that get confused.*

The words listed here have other meanings besides the ones given. Only those meanings that are a possible source of confusion are quoted.

accede consent to, become party to (*I reluctantly acceded to their request*).
exceed go beyond (*You are always exceeding your budget*).
succeed achieve what is aimed at (*She succeeded in passing her exams*); to follow on or come next after (*What succeeded was a disaster*); attain a position after someone else (*Prince Charles will succeed his mother*).

accept to receive willingly (*We accepted the invitation*).
except to exclude (*They excepted Lisa from the invitation*).

access means or right of entering (*Access was prohibited*).
excess the state of having more than needed (*There was an excess of wine*).

activate to make (a thing) active, make it start working (*By pressing the button he activated the lift*).
actuate to motivate (a person) (*He was actuated by ambition*).

adoptive that adopts or is adopted (*The adoptive parents were very supportive*).

adopted that which has been adopted (*The children were adopted*).

adhesion and **adherence** both mean 'sticking (to)', but **adhesion** is used in the literal sense (*the adhesion of tiles to the wall*) and **adherence** in the sense of sticking to a plan, belief or cause (*adherence to one's principles*). The corresponding adjectives are **adhesive** (*adhesive tape*) and **adherent**. Both of these may be used as nouns: an **adhesive** is a sticky substance, and an **adherent** is a supporter (*of a political party* etc.) The verb is **adhere**.

admission and **admittance** mean 'permission to enter', but **admission** is the more normal word, **admittance** the more official (*He was refused admission to the building. No admittance except on business*).

adverse opposed, unfavourable. An *adverse reaction* to a proposal is one that is hostile.

averse unwilling, reluctant, disinclined (*He's not averse to the idea*). Both words are followed by **to**. Note that **averse** cannot be applied to a noun: *adverse comment*, not *averse comment*.

affect (verb) influence, act on (*How has his death affected her?*); pretend (*He affected not to be concerned*).

effect (noun) result (*His warning had no effect*); state of being operative (*To put a plan into effect*).

effect (verb) bring about, achieve, accomplish (*They effected an escape*).

A common mistake is to use **effect** (verb) for **affect**. Either *Ill health has affected* (not *effected*) *his career* or *Ill health has had an effect on his career*.

affection tender attachment (*Her affection was touching*).

affectation insincerity or unnatural behaviour (*His affectation lost him many friends*).

allude mention indirectly (*He alluded to his bad behaviour*).

elude escape (*I eluded my pursuers*).

already before a particular time (*When we arrived the show had already started*).
all ready all prepared (*The cutlery is all ready on the sideboard*).

alternate (adj.) first one, then the other, in turn (*The two caretakers work the night-shift on alternate weeks*; i.e. each has one week on, then one week off).
alternative (adj.) available in place of another; affording a choice (*There is an alternative method*).
The same distinction applies to the corresponding adverbs **alternately, alternatively.**

altogether completely; on the whole (*I forgot altogether*).
all together all at the same time or in the same place (*Parcel them all together*).

always at all times (*He is always helpful*).
all ways (in) every possible way (*We've tried all ways*).

amiable friendly and inspiring friendliness. (Applied only to people.)
amicable in a friendly spirit. (Applied to things; e.g. *an amicable agreement, meeting, arrangement*, etc.)

amoral outside the sphere of moral judgement (*Babies and animals are amoral*).
immoral positively wrong (*Stealing and fraud are immoral*).

appraise form a judgement about. *To appraise a problem is to evaluate it.*
apprise inform. *To be apprised of a problem is to be told about it.*

aural refers to ears and hearing (*The bat's aural apparatus is very acute*).
oral refers to the mouth (*I never do well in oral exams*).
The words are pronounced the same.

authoritarian demanding obedience (*We found the leader too authoritarian*).

authoritative speaking with acknowledged authority (*It is an authoritative account*).

bathos an anticlimax; a ludicrous descent from the very important to the trivial (*How can the poet be unaware that he descends to bathos?*).

pathos the quality that evokes pity (*The pathos at the end of the play was unbearable*).

beside by the side of (*Sit beside the fire*).

besides in addition to, except (*No one was there besides us*). Also moreover, otherwise (*It will take too long. Besides, I don't think it'll work*).

calendar a list of dates (*Check the calendar and tell me when Easter is*).

colander kitchen utensil for sieving food (*Wash the lettuce in the colander*).

canvas type of cloth for tents, etc. (*We camped under canvas*).

canvass to ask for votes or support (*She's in the streets canvassing for votes*).

capital punishment the death penalty (*Capital punishment is carried out by hanging*).

corporal punishment punishment by inflicting physical pain.

censer (noun) a burner for incense (*The priest swung the censer*).

censor (verb) remove undesirable parts of book, film, etc. (*This is a censored edition*).

censure (verb) blame, condemn. Censor and censure act also as nouns with corresponding differences of meaning. (*She was censured for neglecting her work*).

ceremonial having to do with ritual or ceremony (*a ceremonial occasion, ceremonial uniform*).

ceremonious very formal, polite, punctilious; addicted to ceremony. Found mainly in **unceremonious(ly)**, meaning without politeness.

cereal arable crop; breakfast food (*I never eat cereal for breakfast*).
serial single story appearing in separate instalments (*'Oliver Twist' is the latest classic to be made into a TV serial*).
series set of separate stories featuring the same characters (*This television series has gone on for years*).

childish juvenile, that which should have been outgrown (*childish tantrums*).
childlike innocent, as of a child (*childlike enthusiasm*).

classic (adj.) of the highest class; outstandingly typical (*a classic example of bureaucracy*).
classic (noun) thing of the highest quality (*This novel is a classic*). But **the classics** are the literature of classical antiquity as well as distinguished works of art of other countries or periods.
classical (adj.) characteristic of the literature or art of ancient Greece and Rome (*classical civilization*). The word is also applied to serious music. **Classical** has become a confusingly all-purpose word. As well as denoting ancient Greece and Rome, it became attached to the style that imitated Ancient models in the seventeenth and eighteenth centuries. As a style that elevated form over emotion, it served as the polar opposite of Romantic, then inexplicably became attached to music played at symphony concerts, opera houses, chamber music recitals, etc., which may well be Baroque or Romantic, not Classical. So **classical** can be applied with huge diversity: to Homer (the Ancient Greek poet), to the seventeenth-century French playwright Jean Racine or the eighteenth-century poet Alexander Pope, to the music of the iconoclastic, non-classical composer Charles Ives and to a GCSE course about Ancient Rome.

cohesion and **coherence** both mean 'sticking together', but **cohesion** is usually used of people or things, both in its literal sense (*the cohesion of groups of atoms*) and in the figurative sense (*The team lost its cohesion*).

Coherence is usually applied to thoughts or words, in the sense of capacity to be understood or consistency (*The plan lacked coherence*). The corresponding adjectives are **cohesive** and **coherent**.

compliment (noun) expression of admiration (*pay a compliment*). **Complimentary** tickets are free, courtesy of the management. Also used as a verb (*She complimented me on my cooking*).
complement thing that completes. Used more often as a verb meaning to 'go well with' (*These colours complement each other*).

comprehensible able to be understood (*His ideas were clear and comprehensible*).
comprehensive inclusive of everything, of wide scope (*Jan has taken out comprehensive insurance*).

concave hollowed out inwards (*The object is concave, like the inside of a bowl*).
convex outward curving (*The surface of the eye is convex*).

confidant someone to whom secrets are entrusted (*I only became her confidant recently*). **Confidant**, though still current, is a slightly old-fashioned word particularly associated with drama of the seventeenth and eighteenth centuries when every hero had his **confidant** and every heroine her **confidante**. This is a word that still harks back to its French origin by usually appearing in feminine guide as **confidante**.
confident bold, assured (*I'm confident I can do it*).

contemptible deserving contempt; despicable. A *contemptible remark* is one that causes the hearer to feel contempt for it.
contemptuous expressing contempt. A *contemptuous remark* is one that shows the speaker's contempt for someone or something.

continual always or frequently happening. A car's *continual breakdowns* occur often but are (necessarily) separated by periods of normal functioning.
continuous happening without any interruption. A *continuous flow of water* is incessant.

council assembly, as in *town council, council house*.

counsel advice, as in *counsel of perfection*, i.e. ideal but impracticable advice. The word is also applied to a barrister (*counsel for the defence*) and is also used as a verb meaning 'advise'. Similar distinctions exist between **councillor** and **counsellor**.

credence belief, trust, acceptance. *Give credence to* means 'believe'.

credibility quality of being believable (*The whole story lacks credibility*). The adjective is **credible**, with its opposite **incredible**. Don't confuse **credible** with **creditable** meaning 'deserving praise'.

credulity readiness to believe anything. The opposite is **incredulity**, refusal to believe. The adjectives are **credulous** and **incredulous**.

currant dried grape (*She loves currant buns*).

current flow of water or air (*The current of air was icy*); present, actual (*the current situation*).

deduce establish by reasoning (*I deduced your whereabouts from the noise*).

deduct subtract (*I'll deduct it from your wages*). The noun **deduction** has both meanings.

defective having a defect (*The accident was caused by defective brakes*).

deficient insufficient, lacking, incomplete (*Their diet is deficient in carbohydrates*).

delusion false belief sometimes caused by insanity, opinion or impression (*She suffers from the delusion that she is Cleopatra*).

illusion misapprehension (*He is under the illusion that he will be promoted*).

allusion (indirect) reference (*He made no allusion to his illness*; i.e. he did not mention it).

dependent (adj.) relying on (*He is, alas, dependent on drugs*).

dependant (noun) person who depends on another (*He now has ten dependants to support*).

deprecate express (or feel) disapproval of (*Everyone deprecates violence*). A **self-deprecating** person is self-critical, or modest to a fault.

depreciate fall (in value) (*New cars depreciate rapidly*).

derisive mocking, scornful (*We greeted his arrival with derisive cheers*).

derisory absurdly small, so inadequate as to be ridiculous (*The rise we were offered was derisory*).

desert (stress first syllable) an arid region (*They perished in the desert*).

desert (stress second syllable) leave or abandon (*His parents deserted him*); (usually plural) entitlement, what you deserve (*She got her just deserts*).

dessert (stress second syllable) sweet course (*For dessert we have strawberries*).

desirable worthy to be desired (*a most desirable house*).

desirous motivated by desire (*He was desirous of fame and fortune*).

detract take away (*Electricity pylons detract from the beauty of the landscape*).

distract draw (attention) away from; sidetrack, divert the attention of (*He deliberately distracted me from my work*).

devise (verb, *s* pronounced as *z*) think up (*They devised a new board game*).

device (noun) a gadget, a plan, scheme, trick, etc. (*What is that device for?*)

disinterested impartial, free from self-interest. To *take a disinterested view of a matter* is to have no regard for one's personal interest (i.e. advantage).

uninterested not interested (*The boss was uninterested in our working conditions*).

Sadly dictionaries now accept that **disinterested** can carry both meanings. Although this is a useful distinction lost, it means that the positive noun **disinterest** can be used rather than the bland **lack of interest**.

distinct clearly noticeable. A *distinct smell of burning* is a definite, unmistakable one.
distinctive distinguishing, characteristic, peculiar to one thing. (*The distinctive smell of gas distinguishes gas from anything else*).

disused no longer in use (*The factory was old and disused*).
unused (*s* pronounced as *z*) not yet used (*My canoe was still unused*).
unused (*s* pronounced as *s*) unaccustomed (*We're unused to getting up early*).

economic related to economics, business or industry (*economic crisis, economic up-turn*); reasonably profitable (*economic deposits of oil*).
economical cheap, not expensive (*The car is economical on petrol*).

effective impressive, striking (*an effective performance*); having the power to produce the desired result (*an effective strategy*).
effectual having produced the intended result (of things only) (*The plan came to nothing – it was not effectual*). However, **ineffectual** can be used of people too.
efficient producing results with the least fuss and best use of resources (*an efficient postal system*); capable and competent of doing the work (of people) (*an efficient operator*).
efficacious having the power to succeed in producing a result, often in medicine (*The drug was efficacious*).
All four words apply to that which has an effect.

elder/eldest of people only and mostly within families. (*She was the elder sister*).

older/oldest more general usage of people and things (*The older of the two men chose the oldest of the three cars*).

elicit to bring or draw out (*To elicit the facts was difficult*).
illicit illegal, unsanctioned (*Laundering money is illicit*).

elusive hard to catch, grasp or identify (*The fragrance was slight and elusive*).
illusive/illusory deceptive, unreal (*Sadly, his hopes were illusory*).

emigrate leave one's native country to settle in another (*She emigrated to Australia*).
immigrate come to a foreign country to settle there (*He immigrated here from Australia*).
migrate (said of people and especially of birds) leave one area and settle in another (*The refugees migrated south*).
The nouns **emigrant, immigrant** and **migrant** reflect the same differences of meaning as the verbs.

eminent prominent, outstanding (*He's an eminent surgeon*).
imminent about to happen, threatening (*The collapse was imminent*).

emotive arousing emotion. An *emotive issue* gives rise to strong feelings.
emotional showing, or inclined towards, strong feelings (*She is a very emotional person*).
If a singer or actor performs with strong feeling and affects the audience, the performance might be referred to as **emotional** or **emotive** for much the same reasons, but this does not mean that the words are interchangeable.

empathize possess the imaginative power to identify with someone (*She could empathize with the gorillas – get right under their skin*).
sympathize feel sympathy for the feelings or situation of someone (*She could sympathize with the plight of the refugees*).

ensure make certain (of). (*We may ensure the success of a venture by ensuring that everything is fully prepared*).

insure guarantee against risk, harm or loss by paying **insurance**. (*She insured her car*).

assure make (person) sure or confident (*I was assured that there was nothing to worry about*).

equable pleasantly free from extremes (*an equable climate, an equable temperament*).

equitable fair and just (*an equitable distribution of the spoils*).

especially in particular, particularly, pre-eminently (*This room is especially beautiful*).

specially for a particular purpose (*The room has been specially decorated for the party*). **Special** also means 'out of the ordinary'.

exceptional unusual (*The heat was exceptional*).

exceptionable open to objection (*His behaviour was not exceptionable*). The more usual form is the negative **unexceptionable**.

exhausting very tiring (*The work was exhausting*).

exhaustive covering all possibilities (*an exhaustive investigation*).

fictional belonging to fiction, i.e. to literature. A *fictional character* is a person in a novel, etc.

fictitious not genuine. A *fictitious name* is an assumed one.

flaunt display conspicuously; show off, as in *flaunt one's wealth*.

flout treat with contempt, as in *to flout the rules* or *to flout someone's authority*.

forcible done by force (*The forcible entry caused damage*).

forceful (of people) powerful, strong (*My father was a forceful speaker*).

formerly in the past (*He was formerly a teacher*).
formally as required by convention or rules, especially those of politeness (*He was formally dressed*).

further additional (*closed until further notice*)
further/furthest and **farther/farthest** both are used to talk about physical distance (*We lived furthest from the station; The farthest planet is Pluto*).

gild cover in gold (*The huge bonus merely gilded the lily*).
guild association of merchants or artisans (*medieval guilds*).
guild has changed its spelling over time. In medieval times a medieval **gild** was spelt that way – or some fourteenth century variant – certainly not **guild**. Over the years the spelling **guild** became established; possibly the 'u' was inserted to affirm the hard 'g', as in 'guilt', though it never happened for the other meaning of **gild**. Now the desire for authenticity means that **gild** is often used for the medieval trade association, though **Guild Hall** remains unaffected.

gorilla large African ape (*Gorillas are gentle animals*).
guerrilla an irregular soldier (*The guerrillas were terrorists, not freedom fighters*).

gourmand greedy person (*He was a bit of a gourmand where chocolate was concerned*).
gourmet connoisseur of food and drink (*To eat wisely you need to be a gourmet*).

historic noteworthy, so as to deserve a place in history (*a historic victory*) or having a long history (*historic houses*).
historical concerned with history (*a historical novel*) or relating to history rather than legend, etc. (*a historical character*).

hoard (noun) (secret) store. (*He kept his hoards in the cellar*). The word is also a verb meaning to save and store up (*He hoards nothing but gold*).
horde large crowd of people or insects (*hordes of demonstrators*).

imaginary imagined, not real (*No need to fear imaginary dangers*).

imaginative inventive, arising from imagination (*The child showed imaginative power*).

incredible difficult to believe, impossible (*The story was completely incredible*).

incredulous showing disbelief (*She was incredulous – the story didn't make sense*).

ingenious inventive, clever (*an ingenious little gadget*).

ingenuous innocent, incapable of deception (*He was frank, candid and ingenuous*).

industrial related to industry in its sense of trade or manufacture (*an industrial dispute, the Industrial Revolution*).

industrious hard-working (*The blacksmith is an industrious worker*).

inquire/inquiry are interchangeable with **enquire/enquiry,** but it is usual for the *en-* forms to be used of asking questions, and the *in-* forms of making investigation. To *make an enquiry* is to ask for information; to *hold an inquiry* is to make an (official) investigation.

lay (transitive verb) place down (*lay a carpet, lays an egg*, etc.). The past form is **laid** (*He laid/had laid a trap*) and the *-ing* participle is **laying** (*The hurricane is laying waste the whole area*).

lie (intransitive verb) recline, rest (*lie sunbathing, lies down*). The past tense is **lay** (*The ship lay at anchor*), the *-n* participle **lain** (*She has lain awake all night*) and the *-ing* participle **lying** (*I found him lying there*).

licence (noun) permission (*driving licence*); excessive freedom (*licence to kill*); a departure from rule or convention (*poetic licence*).

license (verb) give a licence or permit (*to license the car*).

lightening getting lighter (*Lightening his task won't be easy*).
lightning flash of bright light caused by discharge of static electricity (*thunder and lightning*).

loose release or detach (*He loosed the dogs*).
lose fail to keep (*I keep losing my way*).

metre unit of length (*fifty metres long*).
meter instrument used to measure something (*parking-meter*).

mitigate alleviate, moderate, lessen (*His apology mitigated her anger*). *Mitigating circumstances* are those that make an error or crime seem less severe.
militate (against) operate, have effect (against) (*The scandal has not militated against his popularity*).

official (adj.) having authority (*an official letter*).
officious interfering, giving unwarranted help (*He was officious, always poking his nose in*).

partially not completely (*They were partially successful*).
partly in part (*The sculpture was partly in wood, partly in metal*).

practicable capable of being done. A *practicable scheme* is one that can be put into practice. The opposite is **impracticable**.
practical concerned with practice (not theory). A *practical man* is good at doing things; a *practical examination* requires you to do or make something. The opposite is **unpractical** (usually applied to people) or **impractical** (not useful in practice).

practice (noun) An habitual activity or performance (*She made a practice of gong for a long walk on a Sunday*). Can be used as an adjective (*a practice match*).
practise (verb) to perform habitually (*I practise the piano every day*). The difference may be remembered by analogy with **advice** (noun) and **advise** (verb).

The general rule is *s* for the verb and *c* for the noun in otherwise identical words. American English uses **practice** for both noun and verb.

precipitate (adj.) hasty, rash (*a precipitate departure or action*).
precipitous very steep (*a precipitous slope*).

prevaricate respond to a question but avoid being completely truthful (*He prevaricated, not being completely honest*).
procrastinate refuse to deal with something, put off something (*He procrastinated, putting it off for as long as he could*).

prey (verb) bully or frighten (*He preyed on young girls*). Also a noun meaning victim, an animal regularly hunted and killed by another (*Mice are often the prey of owls*).
pray make an earnest request (e.g., to God) (*We prayed that he would come*).

principal (adj.) chief (*one's principal source of income*). It may be used as a noun (*a college principal*).
principle (noun) universal law; state of conduct (*I objected on principle; He would never change his principles*).

prise force with difficulty (*He prised open a container; They will prise the information out of her*).
prize (noun) something of value (*He won a prize for maths*).
pry look or ask inquisitively or impertinently (*He pries into other people's business*).

prostate gland round the base of the bladder (in males) (*He has prostate trouble*).
prostrate lying down (*Being prostrate is his favourite position*).

recourse (noun) source of help or protection (*He had recourse to his lawyer*).
resort (noun) meaning both source of help (*as a last resort*) and place frequented for holidays (*Brighton is a popular resort*). Also a verb meaning to seek help in (*He resorted to violence*).

resource (noun) source of help; expedient (*Determination was their only resource*).

rein put a brake on (*He reined in his horse*).
reign rule, govern (*She reigned over a quarter of the globe*).
rain pour down on (*Confetti rained down on us*).

restive resistant to control. A *restive crowd* is impatient and irritated.
restless unable to rest, fidgety (*The baby gives us restless nights*).

review (noun) survey, examination (*The report is a review of the company's progress*).
revue entertainment consisting of songs and short acts. (*There is a revue at the theatre tonight*).

sceptic (pronounced *sk*) person who tends to disbelieve what he is told (*The sceptics didn't believe the politicians*).
septic infected, poisoned (*Don't let the wound turn septic*).

silicon non-metallic element (found in clay and rocks and in sand) used as semi-conductor (*silicon chips, Silicon Valley*).
silicone chemical often found in waxes, plastics, paints, etc. (*This paint contains silicone*).

sociable liking company. A *sociable person* is friendly and communicative.
social of society or the community (*You lead a busy social life*).

stationary (adj.) not moving (*The car was stationary*)
stationery (noun) paper, pens and other items necessary for writing (*office stationery*).

suit a set of matching clothes, clothing for a particular purpose, (*a two-piece suit, a space suit*), a set of playing cards with pips of the same colour and shape (hence *follow suit*). Also a verb meaning to be fitting for or appropriate to (*The dress suited her*).

suite (pronounced *sweet*) a set of furniture, rooms, pieces of music, and people forming a group of attendants.

yolk yellow part of the egg (*Her egg had a double yolk*).
yoke wooden frame linking two oxen pulling a cart; part of a dress; a burden (*His yoke was light*).

8

Common errors (1) alphabetical

In this chapter you will learn:

*   *about common errors you may come across, sorted into alphabetical order to help you.*

a or **an**? Write **a** before words beginning with a consonant sound (e.g. *a baby, a cap, a knee, a question, a wren, a xylophone*) and **an** before words beginning with a vowel sound (e.g. *an ache, an heir, an old ..., an hour*). The vowel *u* has two sounds: write **a** when the sound is *yoo* or *yor* (*a union, a use, a European*) and **an** when the sound is *uh* (*an usher, an upward ...*). Words that begin with *h* and an unstressed syllable nowadays usually start with **a** rather than **an** (e.g. *a hotel, a historian*), but the use of **an** is not wrong.

ain't is a dialect word and has no place in correct speech or writing.

almost needs positioning carefully. Distinguish between *He almost lost all his money* (= he didn't lose any) and *He lost almost all his money* (= he lost most of it). Do not confuse **almost** (*It's almost all interesting* = nearly all) with **all most** (*It's all most interesting* = all of it).

alright for **all right** is not strictly speaking correct although it is becoming more acceptable.

also is not a conjunction. Add or substitute **and** in *I left my umbrella, also my coat* and in similar expressions when **also** is used to introduce additional information.

alternative used to be applied to one of only two possibilities; it is no longer so limited. It does imply choice, however, and it is illogical, though common, to use it when no genuine choice is implied (*There is no other alternative*) or when other would be correct (*When North Sea oil runs out, we shall need an alternative supply*).

alternative and alternate Alternate should not be used as a synonym for **alternative**. It means taking it in turns, one after the other: *The Chair called on alternate speakers from each side.*

aren't I? is colloquial, and its equivalent **am I not** (as in *Am I not right to say … ?*) should be used in writing.

as how should be **that** in *I can't say as how I agree*, or simply **how** in *He didn't see as how he could help*.

as if is still correct in sentences such as *It looks as if it's going to rain*, and *It seems as if we are in for a long wait*. The word **like** is now generally accepted as an alternative but **as if** is still safer in formal writing.

barely see **hardly**.

between There used to be a rule that **between** should be used when there are only two persons or things and **among** when there are more than two. This is no longer strictly observed, and it is quite normal to hear **between** being used when more than two things are concerned (*Let's switch between channels*; *a pact between these four countries*). When talking about sharing or distributing it is common to find **among** (*Divide it out among yourselves*) and to find **between** when individual people or things are named (*Between the two of us we are well qualified*; *between you and me*). A growing and regrettable tendency in speech in recent years is to use **between** and then, as it were, forget about it: *There are hold-ups between Junction 28 to the Woodall Services –* it's always *between … and*.

bored with or **by**, not **of**.

borrow never means *lend*. He lent me a pen (not *he borrowed me a pen*).

both should not be used of more than two people or things. (*The journey was both long and difficult*).

can denotes ability (*Can you come tomorrow?*) or capability (*Can you play the piano?*); **may** denotes permission (*May I come in?*) or possibility (*I may go away for the weekend*). Because these two sets of meanings often overlap, the two words have become interchangeable in many phrases. However, when capability is the predominant meaning, use **can**: *can you see the point?*

centre round is bad English. A discussion may **centre on** a subject, or **revolve around** it, but not **centre round** it.

compare to or **compare with**? If you liken someone or something to someone or something else, use **compare to** (*She compared the sound to that of a lawnmower*). Otherwise, when examining similarities or differences, use **compare with** (*Compared with Jean, she's more like a sister than a friend*).

comprise of is incorrect; the **of** is superfluous. (*The symphony comprises four movements* or *... consists of/is composed of/has four movements.*)

different from is preferable to **different than** or **different to**. (*The puppies were very different from what we expected; these cars are different from those.*)

doubt that is correct in negative sentences (*I don't doubt that the decision is wrong*), and **doubt whether** in positive ones (*I doubt whether the figures are accurate*).

easy is not an adverb except in a few idiomatic expressions (*go easy, easy does it, take it easy, stand easy, easy come easy go, easy-going*). In other cases use **easily** as the adverb (*I can get there easily in five minutes*).

e.g. means *for example*, and should not be confused with **i.e.** (*that is to say*), which introduces a rephrasing or clarification of the previous statement.

either of can refer to two only (*Joshua didn't see either of the two men*). It must be followed by a singular verb (*Either of the two is possible*).

equally as is an example of duplication of meaning. Use one word or the other (*He is as successful as his brother; He and his brother are equally successful*).

essential deserves to be regarded as an absolute, having no degrees: either something is essential or it is not. If you feel tempted to add words like *fairly, rather, very,* etc. fit the required sense, it is better to replace **essential** by **important, useful,** etc.

etc. means *and other things* and should not be applied to people. It should end with a full stop; there is no need to add a second full stop if **etc.** occurs at the end of a sentence. *And etc.* is incorrect.

fed up (slang) is followed by **with,** not **of.**

fewer or **less?** **Fewer** applies to numbers, i.e. what can be counted (*We need fewer teachers; there are fewer here today*). **Less** applies to quantity, i.e. what can be measured (*The less milk you use, the better*). The common error is to use **less** when **fewer** is correct.

first two, first three, etc., as in *the first two chapters,* makes better sense than the **two first,** etc.

forever (one word) means *continually;* **for ever** (two words) means *for always.* American English uses one word for both senses. *Forever and ever* is ungrammatical.

former, latter must be applied only to one of two people or things. **The latter** strictly applies to the second of two choices; **the former** refers to the first. The terms are often used loosely, in a way that sends the reader back to the preceding sentence to work out what they refer to. You can sometimes rephrase to avoid their use. In *She decided to clear out the attic. The latter was filled with junk,* **latter** is not applied to one of two, and must be replaced by *This* or *..., which.*

guess is an Americanism for *think* which is creeping into the language in the UK. It is not strictly speaking correct in British English, as there is no good reason for saying *I guess I'll go to bed* unless guesswork is needed.

hardly should be followed by **when,** not **than,** when the sense is *no sooner ... than* (*The game had hardly begun when the fog descended*). **Hardly** has a negative meaning and needs no other negative: *I couldn't hardly believe it* is wrong. Say *I could hardly believe it* (or *I couldn't believe it*). The same is true of **barely.**

he is the subject pronoun; **him** is the object pronoun. *He spoke to Cipriano; Cipriano spoke to him.* There is a similar distinction between **she** and **her.**

hopefully means *in a hopeful way* (*We waited hopefully for our results*) but nowadays it is often used to mean *it is hoped* (*Hopefully they'll arrive on time*). Many people do not like this use of the word even though it is increasingly common and it is wiser not to use it in formal writing.

however should be **how ever** when the meaning is interrogative (*How ever did that happen?*).

I is the subject pronoun, **me** the object pronoun. *Darrell and I stayed behind* (not *me*); *she handed me the book* (not *I*).

if or **whether**? Use **if** to introduce a condition (*If you want to come, let me know* = answer required only if you want to come). Use **whether** to introduce an indirect question (*Let me know whether you want to come* = answer required in either event).

into is a preposition (*The car ran into the wall*), but **in to** is correct when *in* is an adverb and *to* a preposition (*Take the tray in to her*) or *to* is part of an infinitive (*They went in to ask about it*). **Into** in the sense of *interested in* (*He's into greyhound-racing*) is colloquial and should not be used in formal writing.

kind is singular, so *this kind* and *that kind* are correct; *these kind* and *those kind* are not. The same is true of **sort**, **type** and **class**.

lend can never be used to mean *borrow*. *I'll lend you my book*, not *I'll borrow you my book*.

less see **fewer**.

like is followed by pronouns in the object-form (*like you and me*, not *like you and I*).

literally means 'in exact accordance with the meaning of the word it applies to' (*The house was literally only five minutes' walk away*). Used correctly it intensifies the meaning of the verb (*He was literally speechless*). When used incorrectly it frequently results in absurdity (*The audience were literally glued to their seats*).

me going or **my going**? Use **my going**, and also **your, his, her, our, their going**, etc. (*They object to her going; I hope you don't mind my saying so*). The use of *me, you*, etc. is wrong here.

neither of means 'not one nor the other of two' and should not be used when more than two is implied (*I saw neither of the two*). With three or more, say **none of**.

nor is correct after **neither** (*neither rhyme nor reason*) but **or** should be used after **no** (*no time or energy*) and **not** (*has not written the minutes or the agenda*). There is no need to repeat the negative by using **nor**.

no sooner ... than, not ... *when* or ... *that* (*No sooner had the band started to play than the lights fused*).

of is sometimes used instead of **have** or its contraction **'ve** (*I shouldn't of said that; he could of hurt himself*). This is wrong: **of** is never a verb.

of or **off**? Use **of** to denote possession or belonging (*A friend of mine painted it; the crew of the cargo ship were evacuated*). Use **off** in many other verb constructions to denote direction or movement (*lift it off; drive off; be off; take off, off the street; turn off, sleep it off*, etc.). Avoid following **off** with **of** (*He stepped off the platform*, not *off of*; *They bought the pears from the old lady*, not *off of*).

on account of means *because of* not *because*. *I stayed at home on account of I was feeling ill* is wrong. The correct version is ... *because I was feeling ill* (or ... *on account of feeling ill*).

onto is still colloquial: **on to** is preferred (*I think he's on to it*). Do not use **on to** if **on** is sufficient. Never use **onto** when **on** is an adverb and **to** a preposition (*Keep right on to the end of the road*) or part of an infinitive (*He went on to say ...*)

ought has the negative form **ought not**, not *didn't ought* (*You ought not to have done it*).

perfect is an absolute quality and is always used on its own, without any qualification such as *more, most, quite, less, utterly* or *completely* (*The weather was perfect; It was a perfect present*). 'Absolute' here means that it either is, or is not: it is not a question of degree. The word must therefore stand alone in the sentence. Other absolute qualities include *unique*, and *simultaneous* (*Her painting is unique*, never *quite unique* or *almost unique*). However, it is permissible, if slightly tautological, to use *quite* or *totally* as an intensifier with either **perfect** or **unique**.

prefer Use **to** not *than* (*I prefer swimming to golf*, not ... *than golf*). Similarly, something is **preferable to** (not *than* or *from*) something else. Also, avoid *more preferable* and *most preferable*.

protest is used as a transitive verb in a few expressions (*protest one's innocence/ignorance*), when it means *affirm*. When it means *complain*, one should use **protest against** ....

quite means both *completely* and *fairly*. The tone of voice makes clear which sense is meant when someone says *I am quite happy*; in writing, there is a need to be more specific, or ambiguity may result.

reason Say **the reason is that** not *the reason is because* or *the reason is due to* (*The reason he phoned was that he was worried*). You can also say **the reason for** but don't add *due to* (*The reason for the accident was carelessness*). **The reason why** used to be considered unacceptable, but this is no longer the case.

relationship to applies to degree of relation; **relationship with** applies to manner of relationship. *What's your relationship to the boy? I'm his father*, but *What's your relationship with him like? Good on the whole.*

scarcely should be followed by **when**, not *than*, when the sense is 'no sooner ... than' (*I'd scarcely finished mending the roof when the rain started*). **Scarcely** has a negative meaning and needs no other negative word: *I scarcely never see him* should be *I scarcely ever see him*.

seeing as should be **seeing that**, but the simpler **as** or **since** is preferable.

seldom is an adverb (*he seldom loses his temper*), not an adjective. In *His visits are seldom*, *seldom* should be **infrequent**.

so as and **so that** The phrase **so as** is used before any infinitive (*to* form of the verb) to express a purpose (*He drove quickly so as to arrive early*). **So that** is also used to introduce a purpose

(... *so that he could arrive early*) but be careful not to leave out *that*.

such is followed by **as** before an infinitive (*He's not such an idiot as to believe that*) or an adjectival clause (*It was such a gale as we'd never known before*) but by **that** before an adverbial clause expressing a result (*He's not such an idiot that he'll believe that*).

suffer with as in *He was suffering with a cold* is colloquial. Use **suffer from** instead.

superior to, not *than*.

teach can never be used to mean *learn*. *I'll teach you to cook* (never *I'll learn you to cook*).

theirs is never spelt *their's*.

themselves is correct; *theirselves* does not exist.

there, their, they're Keep these separate: **there** refers to a place (*Put it over there*) or is used in expressions such as *There is ...* ; **their** refers to possession (*Their money is safe*); **they're** is the shortened form of *they are*.

they is the subject pronoun; **them** the object pronoun. *They were there* (never *them*, or *them boys*).

to, too, two Keep these separate: **to** is a preposition (*He went to Glasgow*) or introduces a verb (*You have to go now*); **too** means *also*, and *excessively* (*Will you come too? No, I'm too tired*); **two** is the number.

try and is often used instead of **try to** in speech; **try to** is better in writing.

we is the subject pronoun; **us** the object pronoun. *We saw him*; *he saw us* (never *us saw*, or *he saw we*).

what is never correct for **which** or that. *These are the books what I have just read* should be *These are the books that I have just read*.

where, were Take care to distinguish between the two: **where** means 'at/to what place' (*Where did I put it? Where are you going?*); **were** is a past tense of the verb *to be* (*We were there with you, remember?*). In formal writing **were** not *was* should be used to express a state of affairs that is contrary to fact

(*She wishes it were finished*, when it isn't), or which is not yet a fact and may never be so (*He spoke as if I were deaf*; *If it were to rain, it would spoil our plans*).

whose, who's Keep these separate: **whose** is the possessive form of *who* (*Whose car is it?*); **who's** is short for *who has* (*Who's eaten my sandwich?*) or who is (*Who's coming to the match?*).

your, you're Keep these separate: **your** means 'belonging to you' (*Is this your bike?*); **you're** is the shortened form of *you are*.
yours is never spelt *your's*.

9

Common errors (2)

In this chapter you will learn:
* *about errors made with participles, position of words, split infinitives, the use of 'should' and 'would', negatives and the subjunctive.*

Ambiguity in the use of participles

The parts of the verb that end in *-ing* or in *-ed*, *-n*, *-en*, *-d*, or *-t* are participles: *walking, laughed, won, bound, slept*.

When you begin a sentence with a participle, make sure you relate it to its correct subject:

▶ *Walking* through the field, the snake bit me. (Who was walking? I, not the snake. 'I' is therefore the subject of the participle, so the sentence should read: Walking through the field, I was bitten by the snake.)
▶ *Running* across the road, the car knocked him down. (The subject should be 'he' – the car wasn't running – so the sentence should read: Running across the road, he was knocked down by the car.)
▶ *Tired* out by a long day's work, the train lulled Samantha to sleep. (Samantha, not the train, was tired, so the sentence should read: Tired out by the long day's work, Samantha was lulled to sleep by the train.)

Ambiguity caused by position of words

Take care where you position groups of words:

▶ Asif was feeding the dog in a bathing costume. (It was Asif who was in the bathing costume, so the sentence should read: Asif, in a bathing costume, etc.)
▶ The deer was shot by the keeper with an injured leg. (Ambiguity. Was it the deer or the keeper with the injured leg? If the former, the sentence should read: The deer with the injured leg, etc.)
▶ We saw a young woman enter carrying a baby and her husband. (The young woman was not carrying her husband as well. The sentence should read: We saw a young woman, who was carrying a baby, enter with her husband.)

Split infinitive

The infinitive is the form of the verb preceded by 'to'. When words come between 'to' and the following infinitive, the infinitive is said to be split. It used to be an absolute rule never to split an infinitive but nowadays the rule is no longer strictly observed. However, in formal writing it is best to avoid doing it if possible:

> I want you *to hold on* tightly. (not 'to tightly hold on')
> She asked him *to go* quickly. (not 'to quickly go')
> You ought of course *to apply*. (not 'to of course apply')
> Will you agree resolutely and wholeheartedly *to support* him? (not 'to resolutely and wholeheartedly support him')

....
Insight
The final example above throws up a rather more complicated case of word order than is implied just by the split infinitive. It's possible to agree resolutely and wholeheartedly or to support him resolutely and wholeheartedly. In one case you

boldly make a statement that you may or may not stand by; in the other you do not waver in your support, although you may or may not have agreed with any enthusiasm. The above example implies the former, but placing the adverbs at the end of the sentence suggests the latter.

An infinitive with a long split is ugly stylistically; avoid cases like: 'I tried to despite all the difficulties complete the project'.

Many writers feel that splitting the infinitive is less awkward, or more forceful, at times than not splitting it:

> They were determined *to boldly go*. (rather than 'to go boldly' or 'boldly to go')
> He wants her *to really try*. (rather than 'really to try' or 'to try really')

Should or would?

If 'ought to' is meant, use *should*:

> You really *should* keep your promise. (= ought to)
> We *should* go to the meeting, but we're too busy. (= ought to)

When 'if' is meant, use *should*:

> *Should* we come, we will arrive early. (= if)
> Tell her to wait, *should* you see her. (= if)

When determination, willingness or wish is meant, use *would*:

> She *would* keep on despite being told not to. (= determination)
> *Would* you take this from me, please? (= are willing to)
> He *would* gladly do it, but he can't. (= willing to)
> *Would* that they were here. (= wish)

If 'ought to have' is meant, use *should*:

> I *should* have written. (= ought to have)
> We *should* have done it at once. (= ought to have)

If 'intended to have' is meant, use *would*:

> He *would* have gone, but he was too ill. (= intended to)
> We *would* have done it for you if you had asked.
> (= intended to)

Negatives

Use only one negative in a sentence to express negative meaning:

> Asra could *not* see *any*. (not 'none')
> We could *not* get *any* water. (not 'no water')
> She does *not* know *anything*. (not 'nothing')
> They were *not* going *anywhere* in particular. (not 'nowhere')

You can express the same meaning by following a positive with a single negative:

> Asra could see *none*.
> We could get *no* water.
> She knows *nothing*.
> They were going *nowhere* in particular.

After a negative, use *or* to express a negative meaning:

> He does *not* visit the cinema *or* the theatre.
> Sharon *cannot* knit *or* sew.
> Harry has *not* skill *or* stamina enough to get into the first
> team.
> He lies, *not* because he intends to *or* is conscious of it, but
> because he cannot help it.

After a negative, use *either ... or* to express negative meaning:

> He did *not* go *either* to the cinema *or* the theatre.
> Sharon *cannot either* knit *or* sew.
> Harry has *not either* skill *or* stamina enough to get into the first team.

After a positive, use *neither ... nor* to express negative meaning:

> He goes *neither* to the cinema *nor* the theatre.
> Sharon can *neither* knit *nor* sew.
> Harry has *neither* skill *nor* stamina enough to get into the first team.

Two negatives make a weak positive:

> Sarah is *not unhappy* to be chosen for the race. (= Sarah is fairly happy, but not completely. Compare with 'Sarah is happy to be chosen ... ')
> I should *not* be *unwilling* to do it. (= I should be quite willing to do it.)
> It is *not unreasonable* to ask him. (= It is quite reasonable ...)
> He is *nothing* if *not* confident. (= He is perhaps overconfident.)

Avoid writing 'never ever' for *never*:

> She will *never* do it again. (not 'never ever'. 'Never' means 'not ever')

The subjunctive

The subjunctive is the form of the verb that expresses something that isn't a fact; something feared true; doubt; supposition:

> If only it *were* true! ('not was')
> I'd go if I *were* you.

Were he to do it, he would be branded a cheat. (not 'was')
Suppose you *were* commanded to go, what would you do?

As we have seen, the third person singular of the present tense always ends in *-s*:

he sleeps; she walks; it jumps.

Although the present subjunctive is used less often than it used to be, it is still found in some formal writing. Its form is the same as the present indicative except in the third person singular, which lacks *s*, with *be* used for 'am, are, is':

She suggested he *write* for a brochure. (not 'writes')
It is better she *walk* slowly at first. (not 'walks')
I requested that you *be* left alone. (not 'are')

Insight

Many languages have a full range of tenses in the subjunctive. In English it has nearly disappeared, so that the cases given above are the only existing instances of the subjunctive having a separate form. Of course the present subjunctive is the same as the infinitive for all persons, but we never notice it because, in most persons, the indicative is, too. So 'She suggested I write for a brochure' finds the first person singular 'write' exactly the same as the indicative: 'I write very few letters now.'

Have fun with language!

1 *Rewrite these correctly:*

Laughing loudly, the noise deafened me.
If the baby doesn't like the milk, boil it first.

2 *Rewrite to remove ambiguity:*

The dog was being beaten by a man with a bunch of roses.
Gurminder was leading the pony in a new pair of shorts.

3 *Rewrite these so that the infinitive is not split, then decide which version you prefer:*

I asked him to slowly walk.
They were commanded to absolutely obey all orders.

4 *Substitute 'should' or 'would' for the words in italics:*

Frankly, you *ought to* leave at once.
Give him this *if* you see him.
Are you *willing to* keep it for me?
You *are willing to* go, but they won't let you.

5 *Correct the following where necessary:*

They do not go to football matches nor cricket matches.
The poor man cannot see or hear.
I have not either the wish nor the will to attend.
I like neither the white dog or the black.
Sam is neither as tall nor as strong as you.

6 *Correct the following where necessary:*

If only he was here!
I'd trust him if I was you.
Jason would be foolish if he was to accept.
He suggested she rings her father now.
If that is the truth, you are lucky.

Part two
Using the language

10

Choosing the right word

In this chapter you will learn:

- *how to avoid tautology, circumlocution, verbosity, euphemisms,*
  unnecessarily formal words, potentially pretentious words,
  'gobbledegook' and 'legalese', and over-used and vogue words
- *about Americanisms, borrowings from other languages and the*
  language of computers.

Words come at us by the billion from all directions: from
newspapers, magazines and books, TV and radio, down the
telephone, across the desks of offices, over the internet, etc. Being
able to choose the right word to suit the occasion – answering the
Who? What? and Why? questions posed in Chapter 1 – is a skill
that is essential to speaking and writing good English. As well as
deciding whether a word is too colloquial to be used, as discussed
in Chapter 1, we also need to consider whether it is the best word –
the word that really conveys the meaning we want it to have.

English is particularly rich in synonyms – words that mean the
same as each other, or almost the same. Many words that have
almost the same meaning carry different emotional overtones and
nuances that enrich and add to what we want to say. It is also the
case that some words have been over-used, stretched to breaking
point by advertisers and other persuaders, or straitjacketed into
the private languages of sociologists, economists and art critics,
or cajoled into use by politicians. Some have simply become
drained of meaning and should if possible be avoided. Consider,

for example, the word *nice*, which is bland and lacking in meaning, and for which synonyms abound. Here are just a few:

nice (of things): amusing, attractive, delightful, pleasurable, enjoyable.
nice (of people): sympathetic, friendly, amiable, congenial, likeable.

Insight

Certainly the casual use of *nice* for anything that the writer approves of is to be discouraged, but it would be wrong to suggest that there are no situations where it can be effective. When Dylan Thomas describes Mrs. Dai Bread One in *Under Milk Wood* with the phrase, 'Nice to be nice', we know just what he means.

And don't forget another much more precise meaning for *nice*: fine or subtle, as in 'a nice distinction'.

You can no doubt think of others. The best way to acquire a wide vocabulary is to read widely.

Words to avoid

In the following sections words have been grouped under headings that take the form of standard linguistic labels. You will find that many overlap with each other. The important thing is not necessarily to be able to name the particular type of usage but to develop an instinct to avoid it.

TAUTOLOGY

A tautology is the use of words which repeat the meaning found in other words already used, as in *I, myself, personally*. In the following list the unnecessary words are in bold and italics:

sad misfortune	*very* necessary
absolutely essential	*puzzling* mystery
widow *woman*	*unexpected* surprise
past history	*new* innovation
separate *out*	*final* completion
final end	at this moment *in time*
free gift	at this point *in time*
necessary requisite	win *out*
essential requisite	bisect *in two*
prejudge *in advance*	mix *together*
actual fact	end *up*
and additionally	face *up*
miss *out on*	as *a matter of* fact
ultimate end	recur *again*
final end	reverse *back*
combine *together*	revert *back*
must *inevitably*	return *back*
general consensus	*true* facts
the consensus *of opinion*	concerning *the matter*
at a time when	in respect of *the matter*
as from	meet *with*
eliminate *altogether*	

Some longer examples:

> It adds *additional* weight ...
> He chose *to select* cheating as his first topic.
> The general run of events *taken as a whole* ...
> The sky grew darker, *but* nevertheless ...
> The two houses are *both* alike.
> There was nobody *at all* ...
> *The reason why* he is fit *is* because he doesn't smoke.

CIRCUMLOCUTION

A circumlocution (also called a periphrasis) is a roundabout way of saying things. A shorter expression is usually preferable, but sometimes a longer expression is more appropriate out of politeness or sympathy:

> 'I wonder if you would mind passing me the salad', instead of the abrupt 'Pass me the salad'.
> 'I should like to say how sorry I am to hear of your misfortune', instead of 'Sorry to hear of your misfortune'.

Circumlocution is obviously related to tautology and verbosity (see below). It is still a common fault in official, business, and scholarly writing.

VERBOSITY

Verbosity means long-windedness. There are sometimes good reasons for using more words than one might in other circumstances. In a speech, a speaker may deliberately avoid using a technical term and choose to use a longer expression to make the matter clear to an audience. Instead of a guide advising visitors to a cathedral to look at the misericords, he might say: 'the ledges under the hinged choir stalls'. A doctor talking to a patient might choose not to use the word 'diverticulitis', but explain it, taking many words.

In general, it is good practice to be as brief as possible without sacrificing clarity.

EUPHEMISMS

A euphemism is the use of an inoffensive word, or one with favourable associations, instead of a word that may offend because of disagreeable or painful overtones.

Euphemisms are justified when used out of respect for, or empathy with, the person addressed. Otherwise, they are best avoided. Used indiscriminately, they take the edge off what is being expressed. The old adage 'Call a spade a spade' is still worth following.

This list should increase your awareness of euphemisms in common use:

pass away/pass on – die	spend a penny/pee – piss, urinate
put to sleep – kill	cloakroom/bathroom – w.c., etc.
perspire – sweat	pre-emptive strike – attack
overweight/stout – fat	final solution – extermination, genocide
disadvantaged – handicapped in some way	protective custody – imprisonment
agent – spy	armed reconnaissance – secret attack
be economical with the truth – lie	People's Democracy – Marxist State
let you go – sack you	
downsize – make redundancies	
take industrial action – strike	
dentures – false teeth	

The last five are examples of political and military euphemisms, evasive in their intention.

Insight

The words for *the smallest room in the house* (an egregious euphemism in itself) constitute a case of euphemisms within euphemisms. *Bathroom*, the normal polite American term, is one stage nearer what actually happens than *cloakroom*, but still spares blushes. However, the normal non-euphemism cited above, *w.c.* (water closet) literally means a wardrobe or small room with water. *Toilet* is frequently used as more polite than *lavatory*, but what does lavatory really mean? Somewhere where you wash! There is, of course, the good old-fashioned term, *privy* – somewhere private, another euphemism! Even more than with sex, language moves from euphemism to rudeness, with only *loo* (a slang word) in the middle.

UNNECESSARILY FORMAL WORDS

The enormous vocabulary of British English allows us to express the same idea in several ways. One way may be more exact than another, as *scarlet* is more exact than *red*. Another way is to be technical: *fractured femur* for *broken thigh bone*.

Many words differ from their synonyms only by being more formal: *commence*, not *begin*; *purchase*, not *buy*; *gratuity*, not *tip*. In some situations, such words sound pretentious, though they may not in others. In certain formal contexts, *endeavour* may be more appropriate than *try*; *beverage* than *drink*.

POTENTIALLY PRETENTIOUS WORDS

An allied motive triggers those who wish to appear better educated than they are. Using long words unnecessarily gives a bad impression and obscures the meaning. This list of potentially pretentious words followed by their simple alternatives may act as a warning to avoid them. Remember, however, that whether or not a word is considered pretentious depends on the person using it and the context.

abode – home	crucial – decisive, critical
acquaint – know, tell	deceased – dead
adjacent – near	deem – think
aggregate – total	desist – stop
altercation – quarrel	dialogue – conversation
anterior – before	dimension – feature, factor
apogee – peak	dispense – give
appellation – name	disrobe – undress
articulate (verb) – express	dwell – live
ascend – go up	edifice – building
ascertain – find out	escalate – increase, intensify
commence – begin, start	eventuate – result
comestibles – eatables, foodstuffs	furnish – give
compact – small	garments – clothes
consensus – general opinion	impecunious – poor
	integrate – combine

locate – discover the place where	perquisite – extra profit or allowance
loved ones – relatives	predicate – found on, base on
low profile (keep a) – lie low	pristine – original, ancient
massive – huge	reside – live
maximize – make as great as possible	sensational – very impressive
methodology – method	simplistic – oversimplified
notify – tell	source (verb) – find
paradigm – pattern, model, archetype	sufficient – enough
	terminate – end
parameter – boundary	track record – record
	utilize – use

Insight

There are two reasons why I would not recommend avoiding these words altogether. It is usually a good idea to vary your vocabulary and, after a couple of uses of *begin* and *start*, *commence* is a welcome visitor. Also some of the words in the above list have slightly different connotations from the simpler alternatives. A *method* is a way of doing something; *methodology* is the system underlying the methods used. The problem is that *methodology* is sometimes used to mean *method* simply to impress. What is most important is to use the words correctly: it is very embarrassing to choose an impressive word and get it wrong – like those restaurants that encourage diners to leave 'gratitudes'. *Tips* would have been safer.

'GOBBLEDEGOOK' AND 'LEGALESE'

This type of language, used in official letters and forms, is traditionally the province of, among others, government employees and lawyers. It uses unnecessarily long and difficult words that can make a letter or application form almost incomprehensible. Difficulty in understanding is caused both by the words and by unnecessary complexity in the grammar. Here are some examples of the kind of words used, followed by simpler alternatives:

assist, facilitate – help	henceforth – from today, from now on
ascertain – find out	applicant – you
formulate – work out, devise	remuneration – pay, salary, fee
consult – talk to	take cognizance of – notice, know, realize
necessitate – need, compel	
be in receipt of – have received	
initiate – begin	utilize – use
terminate – end	supplementary – extra
ancillary – supporting, helping	for the purpose of – for, to

Many of these words overlap with the kind of words mentioned elsewhere in this chapter. The aim of the Plain English Campaign, which started in 1971, is to wipe out 'gobbledegook' and 'legalese' so that ordinary people can understand the language of official forms of every kind, and in recent years they have had some success.

OVER-USED AND VOGUE WORDS

As we have seen, there are fashions in words, as in everything else. Some fashionable words become over-used and lose their power. Wide and watchful reading will alert you to which words are currently being over-used. Vogue words are usually useful, which is why they are in vogue, but they should not be used merely because they are fashionable; there is often an alternative.

achieve	crash
angle	environment
arguably	escalate
astronomical	fantastic
ballgame	feedback
ballpark	get (in 'understand' sense)
brilliant	great
case	horrendous
confrontation	horrible

image	problem
in-depth	productivity
input	profile
integrate	quality (adj.)
lifestyle	real
low profile	really
marginal	scenario
motivate	significant
negative (in 'hostile' sense)	situation
obscene	state
ongoing	syndrome
operation	target
overall	traumatic
parameter	viable
permissive	-wise
positive (in 'favourable' sense)	

Insight

It is interesting to note the relationship between vogue words and their original usage. In many cases fashion takes it outside of its 'real' meaning. 'Obscene' is a very good word to mean 'offensive to decency', but the types of offence it indicates for most users of the word are not spread too widely – 'obscene wealth', for example. At their worst, vogue words and phrases are used redundantly. 'At the end of the day' had its time in the sun, but in 2010 'going forward' gets the accolade for the most frequent use of a meaningless, would-be impressive phrase.

Words to choose with care

AMERICANISMS

In the twentieth century by far the greatest source of new words was from the USA, through the two World Wars (*pin-up*, *nylons*), the Cold War (*brainwashing, hawks and doves*), the Vietnam War (*defoliate, friendly fire, search-and-destroy*), the nuclear bomb (*countdown, fallout, chain reaction*) and the influence of TV and cinema. Some Americanisms can be resisted where an English word exists – *transportation, utilization* and *escalation* all have good English equivalents, and the habit of adding extra prepositions, etc. – *consult with, meet with, talk with, win out* – is also unnecessary and undesirable.

Although we should be chary of adopting Americanisms that merely duplicate existing British English expressions, such as *I guess* for *I think, sidewalk* for *pavement, pants* for *trousers, vacation* for *holiday* and *garbage* for *rubbish*, there are a large number of expressions originating in America that we use today that have been integrated to such an extent into British English that we no longer recognize them as originally American and rightly use them without qualms: *radio, immigrant, teenager, lengthy, to advocate, to locate, to belittle, live wire, third degree, mass meeting* – the list is endless.

The influence of TV and film ensures that Americanisms, some useful and others not, are constantly entering the language to be accepted or rejected according to fashion. Some become fully naturalized, while others fade and vanish. The greater our awareness of this stream, the better we are able to make informed choices about which words to use.

Insight

It is possible to use American terms alongside British to indicate a slight difference in meaning or emphasis: is *I guess* identical to *I think* or *talk with* to *talk to*? If asked the way, I would use *I think* if I was fairly confident and *I guess* if I didn't know, but was choosing the likeliest option – and, of course, neither of them if I really knew the way. The biggest problem with Americanisms is dealing with words that have different meanings in the two countries, especially when the meanings are similar, as in clothes: *vest and pants*, for example, refer to *waistcoat and trousers* on the other side of the Atlantic.

BORROWINGS FROM OTHER LANGUAGES

The vocabulary of English has been enriched through the ages by borrowings from foreign languages, particularly French and Latin. Some borrowings are necessary because they express a concept for which no English word exists. Many of these have become so thoroughly integrated that we no longer recognize them as foreign, except perhaps when we come to spell them. Think of *restaurant* and *café* (French), *flotilla* and *guerrilla* (Spanish), *concerto* and *opera* (Italian), none of which has any direct English equivalent. If we look at a dictionary that gives the origins of words we can be surprised by the number of languages from which we have borrowed – from Hindi-Urdu (*bungalow*, *curry*, *pundit*) to Hebrew, Arabic to Chinese.

In addition to these, there are certain foreign expressions which, because they express useful shades of meaning or are briefer than their English translations, have been adopted but have stayed 'foreign'. Those which have become established include *status quo*, *ad hoc*, *ad nauseam* (Latin) and *fait accompli*, *carte blanche* (French).

Other Latin expressions are often avoidable, but some, such as *bona fide*, *a priori* or *prima facie* can be justified if their user is confident of being understood, and may even be unavoidable in the technical language of the law, or in talking about music, food or art, where French or Italian words are often needed. The use of *per* (for) may sometimes be needed for expressions like *per cent*, *per capita* or *per annum* and may be needed in some types of writing in front of some English words like 'person', 'head', 'hour' or 'day'. It should be avoided, however, in expressions like 'as *per* usual'. Other Latin words which are usually avoidable include *re* (about), *quasi* (almost), *viz* (namely) and *inter alia* (among other things). Some Latin words have English plurals as well as their own: *formulae* and *formulas*, *termini* and *terminuses*, *referenda* and *referendums*, *stadia* and *stadiums*. Both versions are correct, but the modern tendency is to use the anglicized spellings.

Certain foreign expressions are used as a form of showing off, of making the reader or listener feel inferior. This is another form of pretentiousness. Many Anglo-Saxon words have survived alongside their Latin or Norman French equivalent (*freedom* and *liberty*, *robbery* and *larceny*). Often it is the 'good old' Anglo-Saxon word which is considered superior to the borrowed one – in the twentieth century words such as *wireless* and *napkin* were at various times preferred to *radio* and *serviette*. Sometimes, however, it is the longer, more rotund Latin word that people feel impelled to use, to impress their friends or neighbours.

THE LANGUAGE OF COMPUTERS

The necessity for being computer literate has brought a rich new vocabulary into English, most of which comes from America. Words coined in Silicon Valley such as *hard-wired* can already be used in idioms not immediately connected with information technology: for example in genetics: 'the brain is hard-wired for language'. The new verb *to access* has been allowed to acquire a much more general use than its original meaning, although it is much over-used.

Like much other scientific writing, the tendency is to be too technical and it is all too common to find computer handbooks that are largely incomprehensible to the uninitiated. However, it is interesting to note that words which 10 or 15 years ago would not even have been understood by many people outside the computer industry – *service-provider*, *modem*, *formatting*, *disk*, *logging on*, *surfing*, etc. – have, through the rapid spread of home computers, and with the accompanying use of email and the internet, become almost commonplace. To some extent, therefore, some of the simpler language of computers is no longer jargon and illustrates how the passage of time (sometimes even a very short period) can make a huge difference to the acceptability of words.

Have fun with language!

1 *Be honest!*
  a *Which of the tautologies on page 113 are you guilty of using?*
  b *Which of the euphemisms on page 115 do you use most?*

2 *From the list of potentially pretentious words on pages 116–117 pick out five that you think are often used in newspapers, etc., when they need not be.*

3 *Avoid an over-used word.*
  a *Look up the word 'fine' in a good dictionary and make a note of its various definitions.*
  b *Make up three sentences containing the word in its different meanings.*
  c *Exchange the word for another adjective that is more descriptive in each context.*

  Try this process with another word of your choice.

4 *Be aware of euphemisms. A large company in your area is having problems. It is losing money and people are losing their jobs.*
  a *Write a short description of what is happening on the company's behalf, using some of the euphemisms in the list on page 115 (and any others you can think of).*
  b *Now tell someone in your family what is happening using as few euphemisms as possible.*

5 *Find an official letter, e.g. from an insurance company or bank, and underline any words or expressions that might have been more clearly expressed.*

6 *Words that come and go: can you add to the list on pages 118–119.*

10 THINGS TO REMEMBER

1 *Try to avoid tautology, saying the same thing twice. It is often ugly and clumsy and occasionally downright wrong: to repeat something twice (or again), a common enough phrase, actually means to say or write something three times.*

2 *Circumlocutions are a roundabout way of saying what you want, generally very boring, but of use when the subject matter is delicate.*

3 *Similarly euphemisms, replacing unpleasant words with more delicate ones, have their uses when the audience or reader is unprepared for the harsh truth.*

4 *The English language has become much less formal. Therefore standard written English can seem very stilted if too much formal language is used. Again, though, formal language has its place when the situation itself is formal: medical reports, court judgements, award citations, etc.*

5 *Do not use pretentious words unless you are certain of their meaning.*

6 *Language can be used to obscure meaning as well as convey it.*

7 *Use of vogue words is inevitable (we instinctively pick up the speech patterns we hear), but always be on the lookout for excessive use of the same words and for words used as formulae, not with any real meaning or purpose.*

8 *Usually the simple alternative is best, but always remember the overall effect of the style you adopt: a witty mix of the high-flown and the colloquial can be very effective, as any lover of the great US popular songs of the 1930s knows.*

9 A sizeable proportion of our language consists of words that have gained general meaning as metaphors from some specialist activity (see page 148 for more about metaphors). This is happening now with the vocabulary of computers – and the metaphors have the value of freshness.

10 Always remember that every piece of writing is written for someone, whether it be yourself (in a diary), a friend or relation, a workplace superior, a committee or the typical reader of a type of magazine or book. The audience determines what vocabulary is acceptable and desirable.

11

Writing for a purpose

In this chapter you will learn:
- *about different styles of writing: informative, persuasive, advertising, journalistic, combined informative and persuasive, imaginative and biographical.*

Language is of fundamental importance. It is the means by which we express our thoughts and feelings: we build ourselves as we build our language. In words we commune with ourselves, communicate with friends and strangers; writing in particular develops the writer. Language is the chief factor that holds together our culture and our way of life – with its rituals, beliefs, ideas and values. It is also the means of preserving and transmitting knowledge. The daily bombardment of words in the forms of the mass media has an overwhelming influence on our language and on the way we think and feel.

Just as we use one tone of voice for talking and writing to friends and another for strangers, the style of our writing depends on whom we are writing for and why.

Writing to inform

Look at the following three examples:

▶ Roast garlic: Slice each head of garlic in half horizontally. Put them in the roasting tin cut-side up, and pour the olive oil over the top. Season with salt and black pepper. Tuck the sprigs of thyme around the garlic. Bake uncovered in the oven for 30 minutes, then turn them over and continue to cook for a further 20–30 minutes.

▶ The surface tension of a liquid in contact with its vapour diminishes as the temperature rises, and becomes zero at the critical temperature, when the surface of separation between liquid and vapour disappears.

▶ To the north, the low range of hills which slopes down towards Camberwell and the Thames also offers a steep descent on the south side of Dulwich. On these slopes probably grew the white dill flower from which Dulwich gets its name – *Dilewysshe*, 'the meadow where the dill grows'. Another old road leads down from the ridge of these hills, Aspole Lane (1373), later named Red Post Hill from the colour of the signpost which once stood at its summit.

All three pieces are examples of transactional language. The aim of the authors is to convey facts and information, objectively and literally. There are differences of tone and style, as you would expect, between cookery books, scientific textbooks and travel guides, but the words in all cases are factual and clear. We can find this sort of language in news items, handbooks and manuals, business letters, scientific treatises, and technical reports, as well as in guides and textbooks. It is also noticeable that the authors are unobtrusive and anonymous, their feelings, opinions and personalities being irrelevant. Nothing is allowed to come between the reader and the sense of the words.

The style of objective writing varies according to the type of reader the writer has in mind, even though the subject is identical. A nature article written for a wide middle-of-the-road audience differs from that on the same subject written for a smaller, better-informed one because their readers have different tastes and expectations.

In the first of the two following articles the content is straightforward, the style direct and personal, and the facts and information engagingly presented:

> The pretty young thrush, well taught by its mother, dug out the juicy worm from the dried-out soil. It did not enjoy the fruits of its labour, however, for down flew a bright-speckled robber starling and snatched the fat worm from under the young thrush's beak.
>
> Starlings never try to steal from adult birds. I have, though, often seen them rob innocent blackbirds in the same way. Why, I wonder, do starlings prefer to steal rather than hunt for themselves?

Here is the second article, taken from the nature column of a broadsheet newspaper:

> The two thrushes that may be seen in our garden are the song thrush, *Turdus philomelus*, and the missel thrush, *Turdus viscivorus*. The song thrush is the smaller of the two, 9 inches in length compared with 10.5, and is seen more frequently.
>
> At a casual glance the two seem alike, but the missel thrush, as well as being bigger, has bigger black spots on its breast, and white outer tail feathers. It also has a more upright stance than its smaller relative.
>
> The song of the thrush can be easily distinguished from that of the missel thrush or the blackbird by the repetition of each clear loud phrase, often more than twice.
>
> Both thrushes are fond of earthworms. The young are often robbed, when they have dug one up, by the audacious starling, which will perform the same audacious trick on young blackbirds also. Yet why the starling prefers this method of obtaining earthworms, no one has so far been able to understand.

The second article is more impersonal than the first: the writer keeps his distance. This effect is obtained by writing longer sentences, by the impersonal use of phrases such as 'that may be seen' rather than 'that we may see', by the inclusion of the Latin names, and by the use of less common words such as 'distinguish' for 'recognize' and 'audacious' for 'bold'.

Insight

A simple test of the subjectivity of a piece of writing is, obviously enough, the use or non-use of the personal pronouns. In the first piece on the thrush there is much objective descriptive writing, but in the second paragraph personal observation takes over ('I have ... seen ... ') and the final question is put in personal terms ('Why, I wonder ... '). The first person pronoun identifies the writer and his or her views and experiences and, though the second person pronoun ('you') is not actually used, the final question seems personal, with the use of 'I wonder' suggesting private conversation.

Most scientific language, of the sort exemplified in the second extract on page 127 from a school textbook, which is written specifically to teach and inform, is as clear and economical with words as possible. However, one of the temptations is to be long-winded and obtuse, often to the extent of being virtually incomprehensible to the layperson through the use of jargon or even 'gobbledegook'. Here is an example from a book on musical appreciation:

> This dichotomy is explored through multiplanar interjuxtaposition of bivalent (quasi-multivalent) tone clusters with neo-aleatoric material arranged in spaced points, occlusions, anti-points and reflexes ... ambidilectic thematism is highlighted by the organic reantiorientation of paraorganic material.

The language is turgidly mechanical but one imagines that to a musical expert it is comprehensible. One wonders whether perhaps some of the words – *spaced points, occlusions, anti-points* and *reflexes* – might have been expressed in language we could all understand.

Writing to persuade

Writers and speakers who want to persuade an audience to accept their point of view may decide that the best way is to let the facts speak for themselves. They may use objective and literal language, as does this contributor to a local newspaper:

> Of the 258 children who died of head injuries in this region in the last five years, most were playing at the time of the accident. And of these, three-quarters were injured by a motor vehicle. The majority of these accidents occurred close to the child's home, between the hours of 3 p.m. and 6 p.m.
>
> Among the many methods of reducing the number of such accidents, the most effective at present is to slow traffic by building raised obstacles at short distances from each other along the roads in the danger area.
>
> This is expensive, but no parent, nor indeed any other citizen living in the neighbourhood, opposes such use of part of the money collected in taxes. All are only too glad to contribute to a measure that has proved so successful so far.
>
> The search for other measures, perhaps even more effective, is constant. Readers who may have ideas are invited to write to this paper. Be sure to include your full name and address.
>
> One final point. Do please pay more attention to where and when your children play.

The opposite of literal and objective language is subjective and emotional language, where the writer's deliberate aim is to appeal to the feelings and prejudices of the reader. Sometimes the personal feelings and prejudices of the author are all too clear, as in the following passage:

> Can anyone in this hateful modern world of constant wars not associate the colour red with the colour of blood? And can anyone who has witnessed a Spanish bullfight, the most bloodstained and cruellest of all so-called sports, not associate red with the colour of a matador's cape, the cape which he uses to entice the poor already wounded and weakened bull onto his killing sword? No surprise then, that red, the perpetual symbol of danger, death and destruction, is the vilest, most hateful of colours. How anyone can bear to have red in their house, or even more incredibly to wear it, is something I shall never understand.

The author leaves us in no doubt about his opinion both of bullfighting and of the colour red. But his indiscriminate hatred for all things red, to include even the colours of people's houses and clothes, renders his diatribe ineffective.

The effective writer must be sensitive to slight but important shades of meaning and differences of emphasis carried by words which have the same dictionary definition. These differences often stem from different degrees of feeling which have become associated with some words. All words convey sense, but some have emotive overtones which indicate the user's attitude to that sense. Look, for example, at the difference of meaning between the following:

> thin/slim, mistake/blunder, well-known/notorious, strong-willed/domineering, unclear/muddled, faint-hearted/cowardly, freedom/licence, decisive/ruthless, meticulous/finicky, condemn/damn, repetitive/monotonous.

The first word in each pair is neutral; the second conveys an additional sense of approval or disapproval. These overtones are particularly important in the language of persuasion such as we find in political speeches and the world of advertising.

ADVERTISING

Perhaps the ultimate in persuasive language, advertising is concerned to create an atmosphere, influence attitudes, project a product style and sell it to you. There are many very clever and successful examples of the wording of advertisements. However, like the photographs, drawings and films they accompany, they are usually intended to suggest a mood rather than to stand up to close linguistic scrutiny. There is something lulling in the frequent use of words like *modern*, *perfect*, *powerful*, *lasting*, *best*, *finest*, *smooth*, *luxury*, *exclusive*, *natural*, *stylish*, *new improved*, *real*, and many of these words have lost a lot of meaning in their over-use.

Nowadays the Advertising Standards Authority is there to protest when the wording is deliberately misleading, so that the word *organic*, for example, is supposed to imply certain factually verifiable qualities. Nevertheless, we do language a disservice if we stop thinking about what the words mean. It is not pedantic to ask what the word *only* is doing in 'only £99', and realize that *softer*, *whiter*, *better* are meaningless unless they answer the question 'than what'? The language of advertising is in fact an art form of its own.

Journalism and the mass media

Writers and speakers seeking to persuade others of their points of view have to choose between the use of objective, literal language and subjective, imaginative language. The material that bombards us daily in the newspapers and on radio and TV provides us with innumerable examples of both styles. The style adopted by a journalist or reporter depends entirely on the purpose of the article and on the audience.

The popular press believes strong sensations expressed in strong language sell newspapers. The tabloids with their 'shock' headlines, prefer colourful, usually short, often slangy expressions that convey emotional overtones at the expense of a reasoned view of the facts. The aim is to startle and shock and the means is often by cajoling, with the use of 'sensational' words and phrases:

> *shock* (surprise), *slash* (reduce), *soar* (increase), *probe* (inquiry), *dash* (rapid journey), *tragic* (very sad), *blast* (criticism), *quit* (resign, retire), *row* (disagreement), *rap* (rebuke), *bombshell* (unexpected event), *epic* (very unusual).

Such words make for lively, action-packed writing; large black headlines and exclamation marks serve their purpose in attracting attention. Whether they accurately reflect the events they purport to describe, or over-sensationalize them, or whether useful strong words are made to lose their power by being applied inappropriately, is another matter. If a darts match is *epic*, what word is left for an important human struggle?

Sports journalism, especially the reporting of football, has some expressions all its own which illustrate how words can be used to convey the drama of the occasion in telling the story:

> An under-hit back-pass gifted Gabriel Batista the opener; the Argentine robbed a dozing Henning Berg ... to set up

Abel Balbo for the second; City conceded a goal then denied them the chance of opening the gap; a long hanging cross ... a punched clearance; fired home ... hit the woodwork ... rattled the crossbar, snatched back from the jaws of defeat, etc.

Journalists have to keep firmly focused on the tastes and expectations of their readers, and this governs their choice of facts, information, remarks and comments and the language they use. The style may be thoughtful and interpretative, openly offering a reasoned view of the facts and information, followed by carefully considered suggestions about what will or should happen. It may be emotive and persuasive, trying to support a point of view already decided upon and presenting it in language calculated to appeal to the emotions of the readers.

The language of good journalism is crisp, clear English, written in direct and digestible sentences and is often found in the leader columns of the broadsheets and in the language of radio and TV news bulletins and documentaries.

Writing to inform and persuade

When scientists write for the educated layperson, they often use a language that is precise and economical yet with subjective undertones, forming a careful blend of the objective and the emotional, as they seek to persuade us of their opinion. Here is one such passage:

> *Nature, we have come to understand, is not a rigid juxtaposition of individual creatures to be stamped and labelled, transplanted and exterminated, but a constantly moving, flowing complex of myriads of different varieties and forms from which nothing can be isolated, not even man. Every organism is linked with the others in a network of the most delicate, precisely adjusted relationships. Every single-celled organism, every insect and every bird, plays its role in the world of phenomena; each gives*

*the other its cue. Man is part of the arterial system, just as much
as every animal and every plant; the laws of nature apply to him
too, and if he were not connected with the stream of all life on
earth he would be sentenced to death like a tree whose roots
have been cut off.*

(Herbert Wendt, *The Road to Man*)

Here is another example:

Man the Destroyer: the last 400 years

*For hundreds of thousands of years, ever since man became a
man, he killed animals for food and clothing, as well as to protect
himself. Only in the last 400 years, however, has he – mostly
for profit and sometimes for sport – destroyed animals in such
numbers that many species have become extinct and many
others are in imminent danger.*

*The great massacre of the North American bison (popularly
called the buffalo) is too well known even to mention here. But
during the same period, i.e. from the early 18th century to 1870,
the pronghorn antelope, one of the oldest American inhabitants,
was reduced from 40 million to 19,000.*

*North America has indeed the blackest record of all. By 1914,
she had completely exterminated these mammals: Arizona elk,
eastern elk, eastern forest bison, giant sea mink, the California,
Texas, and plains grizzly bears, eastern puma, plains grey wolf,
Badland bighorn, and these birds: Calrader duck, great auk,
passenger pigeon, heath hen, Carolina parakeet.*

*The story of the extinction of the passenger pigeon shows what
man can really do when he tries. A single flock often numbered
2,000 million birds. When they flew south in their autumn
migration they clouded the skies, filling them for three days on
end. As they passed they were slaughtered in such numbers that
farmers drove their pigs journeys of up to 100 miles to fatten
them on the carcasses. Shot, netted, and knocked from the trees*

in which they roosted, more numerous, seemingly, than the leaves themselves, they were finally exterminated, incredible though it sounds. The last passenger pigeon died in Cincinatti Zoo in 1914.

What put the final nail in the coffin was not the gun and the net, but the simultaneous destruction of the forests they needed for food and shelter.

(James Shelton)

The facts on which this article is based appear to have been carefully researched and are presented objectively. A telling contrast is made in the first paragraph between man's need to kill for food and his recent wanton destruction of whole species. This contrast succeeds in engaging our sympathy simply by stating the facts. The second paragraph uses a trick worth noting. The author mentions the extermination of the buffalo at the same time as saying it is too well known to merit attention! In the same detached tone, the third paragraph lists the creatures man has wiped out, a list all the more moving because not many of his readers would have any idea of how many had perished. To ram home his message, which neatly complements that of Herbert Wendt, the author details the sad story of the passenger pigeon, thus making us wonder exactly how the other species on the list would also have suffered. Thus the article illustrates the effective use of a blend of factual and emotive language.

In the two extracts that follow, the authors, while objectively presenting the facts, take a highly personal and emotive approach, with the frequent use of 'I' and 'we' to persuade their readers of the dangers we are dealing with and to draw us into the argument. As you read, compare their styles for objectivity and ask yourselves how successful their particular styles are in persuading you.

Do not suppose that I am advocating the abandonment of chemical control. We owe a great deal to chemists who have given us methods of controlling the various pests which plague

*our lives. We have only to think of the value of antibiotics
in controlling infectious disease, or of DDT in controlling
malaria (though even here awkward and originally unforeseen
consequences are cropping up in the shape of resistant bacteria
and mosquitoes). What I am against is, and here I speak for
the great body of ecologists, naturalists, and conservationists –
what I deplore is the advocacy and practice of mass chemical
treatment as the main method of pest control. On the contrary,
although chemical control can be very useful, it too needs to be
controlled, and should only be permitted when other methods
are not available, and then under strict regulations and in
relation to overall ecological planning.*

(Sir Julian Huxley)

Dangerous road

*It is more than clear that we are travelling a dangerous road ... We
are going to have to do some very energetic research, research
on other control measures, that will have to be biological, not
chemical. Our aim should be to guide the natural process as
cautiously as possible in the desired direction rather than use
brute force ...*

*We need a more high-minded orientation and a deeper insight,
which I miss in many researches. Life is a miracle beyond our
comprehension, and we should reverence it even when we have
to struggle against it ...*

(C.J. Briejer)

Imaginative writing – descriptive and narrative

We finally come to imaginative writing. Found in novels and short
stories, travel books, biographies and many other genres, it embraces
a mixture of styles. In one passage description may predominate; in
another, narrative; in another, character drawing. What separates it
from other sorts of writing is the use of the author's imagination to

shed a new light on something. Here is a passage from a short story, *The Young Couple*, by Ruth Prawer Jhabvala:

In the morning, after Naraian had gone, Cathy wandered by herself through their two rooms and out onto the roof in her flimsy nylon nightie, yawning and plaiting and unplaiting her long blond hair. Sometimes she looked down into the courtyard to see the men shaving, servants lighting fires, sometimes at the birds wheeling round and round the dome of the mausoleum. So early in the morning everything was still pastel coloured – the sky a pale washed blue, the trees a misty green – all the things that later would become violent and hot. Cathy ate a bit, read a bit, let the hours slip by happily till she saw Naraian again. Some time during the morning the sweeper-woman came to clean – thin, cheerful, battered but gaudy, with big silver anklets and very white pointed teeth; there was no other language but smiles and nods by which she and Cathy could communicate so they made what they could of those. Actually, the sweeper-woman swept very badly indeed, but since they seemed to have established such friendly relations, Cathy felt shy to point this out to her, though Naraian did (rather too rudely and loudly, Cathy thought), but the sweeper-woman never seemed to mind; on the contrary, she showed her pointed teeth wider, whiter than ever.

The seemingly casual but carefully selected details in this passage are so vivid that we are able to feel we are present. Not only that: the details are seen through Cathy's eyes and so we are made aware of the kind of young woman she is, and of her relationship with Naraian, her husband.

In this next extract from a travel book, *Twilight in Italy*, D.H. Lawrence lets his imagination play so powerfully over the scene that it is transformed into something rare and wonderful.

It is the Spring

Meanwhile the Christmas roses become many. They rise from their budded, intact humbleness near the ground, they rise up, they throw up their crystal, they become handsome, they are

heaps of confident, mysterious whiteness in the shadow of a
rocky stream. It is almost uncanny to see them. They are the
flowers of darkness, white and wonderful beyond belief.

Then their radiance becomes soiled and brown, they thaw, they
break and scatter and vanish away. Already the primroses are
coming out, and the almond is in bud. The winter is passing away.
On the mountains the fierce snow gleams apricot gold as evening
approaches, golden, apricot, but so bright that it is almost
frightening. What can be so fiercely gleaming when all is shadowy? It
is something inhuman and unmitigated between heaven and earth.

The heavens are strange and proud all the winter, their progress
goes on without reference to the dim earth. The dawns come
white and translucent, the lake is a moonstone in the dark hills,
then across the lake there stretches a vein of fire, then a whole,
orange, flashing track over the whiteness. There is the exquisite
silent passage of the day, and then at evening the afterglow, a huge
incandescence of rose, hanging above and gleaming, as if it were
the presence of a host of angels in rapture. It gleams like a rapturous
chorus, then passes away, and the stars appear, large and flashing.

Meanwhile, the primroses are dawning on the ground, their light
is growing stronger, spreading over the banks and under the
bushes. Between the olive roots the violets are out, large, white,
grave violets, and less serious blue ones. And looking down the
hill, among the grey smoke of olive leaves, pink puffs of smoke are
rising up. It is the almond and the apricot trees. It is the Spring.

It is not an inanimate Lake Garda landscape Lawrence is
describing, but a living organism. Everything is imbued with a
wonderful life of its own: the Christmas roses rising from their
'humbleness' near the ground, the snow, the 'strange and proud
heavens', the passage of the day and evening, the primroses, the
violets, the blue less 'serious' than the white, the olive leaves,
the almond and apricot trees. This is the creative imagination at
its most magical. Lawrence imagines the natural features of the
landscape as having human feelings: they are personified.

The final extract in this chapter is a narrative one, taken from William Golding's *The Inheritors*, in which the author's powerful imagination enables him to enter the life of the Neanderthals who vanished some 40,000–30,000 years ago, wiped out, apparently, by hunter-gatherers from Africa and the Middle East:

Over the sea in a bed of cloud there was a dull orange light that expanded. The arms of the cloud turned to gold and the rim of the moon nearly at the full pushed up among them. The sill of the fall glittered, lights ran to and fro along the edge or leapt in a sudden sparkle. The trees on the island acquired definition, the birch trunk that overtopped them was suddenly silver and white. Across the water on the other side of the gap the cliff still harboured the darkness but everywhere else the mountains exhibited their high snow and ice. Lok slept, balanced on his hams. A hint of danger would have sent him flying along the terrace like a sprinter from his mark. Frost twinkled on him like the twinkling ice of the mountain. The fire was a blunted cone containing a handful of red over which blue flames wandered and plucked at the unburnt ends of branches and logs.

The moon rose slowly and almost vertically into a sky where there was nothing but a few spilled traces of cloud. The light crawled down the island and made the pillars of spray full of brightness. It was watched by green eyes, it discovered grey forms that slid and twisted from light to shadow or ran swiftly across the open spaces on the side of the mountain. It fell on the trees of the forest so that a faint scatter of ivory patches moved over the rotting leaves and earth. It lay on the river and the wavering weed-tails; and the water was full of tinsel loops and circles and eddies of liquid cold fire. There came a noise from the foot of the fall, a noise that the thunder robbed of echo and resonance, the form of a noise. Lok's ears twitched in the moonlight so that the frost that lay along their upper edges shivered. Lok's ears spoke to Lok.

'?'

But Lok was asleep.

Both Lawrence's and Golding's extracts are descriptive. Both authors use their creative imagination to achieve their effects. But while Lawrence's piece is filled with the wonder and joy of the beauty that surrounds him, Golding's, as seen through the eyes of Lok, is filled with unease and menace.

Biography – character drawing

Unlike writers of fiction, writers of biographies have to be able to bring to life, through their imagination, a 'real' person or subject. They may use any facts or information they can lay their hands on to compose their account: for example, the subject's own writings, diaries, letters or interviews; official historical records of the subject's life and achievements; memories of friends, family or contemporary witnesses; photographs and portraits; even domestic laundry bills and other details.

The biographer decides on the purpose and point of view of the biography. Is it to present as balanced and objective a picture of the person as possible? Is it to set right what the biographer perceives to be an incorrect view of the truth? In the case of a biography of a dear friend or someone much admired, should the biographer concentrate on the good and praiseworthy and gloss over the rest? (When a biography idealizes or idolizes its subject too much, a fault from which many biographies suffer, it is labelled 'hagiography'.)

Biographies have always been written about all kinds of people: not only kings, statesmen, soldiers and poets, but also actors, sportsmen, singers and even criminals. The public's curiosity for the details of other people's lives is insatiable.

Here is an extract from a modern biography of the first great dictionary maker, Dr Samuel Johnson (1709–84), by John Wain, himself a poet, novelist and critic.

Langton was admitted, presumably by Frank Barber [Johnson's black servant] and asked to wait. When Johnson came down and greeted him, the youth's first reaction was one of amazement and shock. As he later told Boswell, he has formed a mental picture of Johnson as a 'decent, well-dressed, in short, a remarkably decorous philosopher. Instead of which, down from his bedchamber, about noon, came, as newly-risen, a huge uncouth figure, with a little dark wig which seemed scarcely to cover his head, and his clothes hanging loose about him'.

This disconcerting impression was something Langton shared with virtually everyone meeting Johnson for the first time. The artist Hogarth, happening to call on Richardson at a time when Johnson was also visiting him, was shown into a room where Johnson was standing by the window, absorbed in his thoughts; as usual when in this state, he was twitching, rolling his frame about, and making strange sotto voce noises, and Hogarth assumed that this was a poor idiot to whom the charitable Richardson was giving shelter. When their host arrived, the 'idiot' moved forward and began to speak, so forcefully and eloquently that the thought crossed Hogarth's startled mind that he was witnessing a case of divine inspiration of the insane.

This account of a meeting with the great man is based on much original research. The reader gets a superb picture of Johnson's appearance and character, not through the biographer's eyes but through those of two of Johnson's contemporaries, which makes the picture all the more convincing.

Have fun with language!

1 *Check a cookery book for a simple recipe and make a note of the simple and objective language it uses.*

Now write a simple recipe of your own.

2 *Record and analyse an advertisement for one of the following products, looking particularly for emotive and persuasive words, expressions of dubious honesty or least unverifiable fact, clichés, jargon, etc.*

   a *a new music album – classical or modern*
   b *a holiday*
   c *a new type of food or drink*

Now try and make one up for yourself!

3 *Find a report of a football match in a tabloid and in a broadsheet newspaper and compare and analyse the headlines and the story.*
Write an imaginary account of a similar match – choosing your sport.

4 *Scan a broadsheet and a tabloid for two articles about the same subject (e.g. the latest genetic discovery or political row) and compare their headlines, styles of writing, etc.*

How does each one seek to inform or persuade? Do they achieve their intention?

10 THINGS TO REMEMBER

1 *Writing communicates meaning, but meaning in different forms. The purely factual and impersonal can be found in, for instance, an old-fashioned recipe – modern celebrity cooks have so much personality it spills into the saucepan!*

2 *It is not necessary to indicate a personal point of view, but many effective pieces of writing develop a viewpoint or an argument with the support of facts and evidence.*

3 *Persuasion can often be helped by using words that have an emotional weight alongside their literal meaning; for instance, disapproval can be conveyed by using* blunder *instead of* mistake.

4 *Similarly – this can be found particularly in the language of politics – the degree of achievement or failure can be enhanced by using words of greater intensity:* triumph *for* success, disaster *for* failure.

5 *Advertising lends itself to words of generalised approval, useful enough in that context, but not to be recommended in other forms of writing.*

6 *We still tend to think of journalism in terms of 'tabloid' and 'broadsheet', terms literally based on the size of the newspaper, but representing two different approaches. Nowadays only the* Daily Telegraph *of the four major broadsheets retains the format, but it is convenient to refer to* The Times, *the* Guardian *and the* Independent *in that way.*

7 *To be convincing a persuasive piece must have more than a passion to persuade. The piece on the colour red is a good example of a writer so over-persuaded himself that he cannot persuade others.*

8 *The purpose of the writing may not be something to be quantified by the understanding of the readers or the extent to which they are persuaded. The purpose may be as simple (and as complicated) as to amuse, entertain or delight.*

9 *Selection of details is all-important in creating everything from characters to atmosphere, from a beautiful scene to a terrifying monster.*

10 *Biography is more than an accumulation of facts. The good biographer must have a perspective on his or her subject. In autobiography this can have appalling consequences when the writer (and subject) has a perspective blighted by self-love.*

12

A writer's tools

In this chapter you will learn:
- *how imagery is created by similes, metaphors and other techniques.*

It is quite possible to enjoy reading a piece of writing without being conscious of the particular skills that have gone into its making, just as one may enjoy a meal without knowing anything about cookery. But enjoyment is deepened if it additionally involves some awareness and recognition of the skill, care and selectivity exercised by the writer. The following sections are therefore intended to demonstrate some of the tools of the trade. A knowledge of how they can be used should enrich your reading experience – and also help to make your own writing more effective.

Simile

A simile is a comparison of two different objects with one thing in common – the point of comparison. In the simile *He went as white as a sheet* the two things compared (*He, sheet*) are unlike, except in the point of comparison, whiteness. A simile is usually introduced by *as* or *like*. Its purpose is to clarify or illustrate, often by introducing a visual element:

> Money is like muck, not good unless it be spread.

Similes are found in everyday speech:

> He was as happy as a dog with two tails.
> The news spread like wildfire.

Very often they are clichés, to be avoided like all over-used expressions, though with a little imagination they can make writing vivid:

> She bit into her toast as if it were a personal enemy.

They can also be used to add meaning:

> Although he is already a millionaire, he has much enjoyed acquiring a national newspaper – like a boy with a new train-set.

The simile here neatly summarizes a range of attitudes and behaviour.

....

Insight

Many words are emotive, as mentioned before, and it is as well to respect this when choosing similes. For instance, if you come across a large and beautiful building unexpectedly, it's unwise to write, 'Across the valley it loomed as large as a tower block.' Tower blocks get a bad press, they are not known for beauty and, though the comparison on grounds of size is valid, some of this sense of ugliness will attach itself to the building you describe in the minds of your readers. Of course, if you are doing this for a deliberate effect, possibly humorous, that's fine, but, done unthinkingly, it can harm your writing.

In fact, quite subtle effects can be gained by this comparison of contrasts. Irving Berlin wrote in his song *Cheek to Cheek* of his cares disappearing 'like a gambler's lucky streak'. You want cares to disappear, but the gambler wishes his streak

(Contd)

to continue, and the overall effect is to suggest that the singer (Fred Astaire, as it happens) has less solid ground for optimism than he thinks.

Metaphor

Metaphor is more subtle and persuasive than simile. It too works by comparison, but this is implicit rather than stated, and the introductory *as* or *like* is omitted. Metaphor is exemplified in *He towers above his contemporaries*: this implies a comparison between *he* and *a tower*, in that both stand out prominently, and there are other possible implications – towers are usually strong, or make people feel small. But these points of comparison are not spelled out; the reader has to deduce them. The meaning is therefore more complex and interesting, allusive rather than explicit.

Metaphor is also more compressed than simile because of the element of identification between its components (he *is* a tower, not just *like* one).

Metaphor is widely, often unconsciously, used in daily speech, and is seen in the difference between the literal and figurative use of words:

literal: The escorting ships laid a smoke-screen to hide their position from the enemy.
figurative: His explanation was a smoke-screen of lies.

The imagery (as the name suggests) creates a picture.

Like simile, metaphor can easily degenerate into cliché: *tip of the iceberg, grind to a halt, food for thought, hit the nail on the head, a dog's life, wild goose chase, old hat, tongue in cheek, bite the dust,* etc.

Properly used, however, it is a rich resource for varied and powerful expressions.

Metaphor often has a brief 'snapshot' effect:

> The conversation lapped on in little wavelets.
> A fountain of sparks shot high into the air.
> They were inundated with offers of help.

In developed prose, metaphor may be extended, as it is in this description of a mouse-like woman:

> *... she was so small and silk and quick and made no noise at all as she whisked about on padded paws, dusting the china dogs ... setting the mousetraps that never caught her; and once she sneaked out of the room, to squeak in a nook or nibble in the hayloft, you forgot she had ever been there ...*
>
> (Dylan Thomas, *A Prospect of the Sea*)

In its most heightened form, when prose comes close to the intensity of poetry, metaphor is not a decoration but a fused-together, organic part of meaning, as it is in the passages from D.H. Lawrence and William Golding in Chapter 11.

At the other extreme, insensitivity to the pictorial element in metaphor may produce the incongruity of the mixed metaphor:

> He has other irons in the fire, but he's playing them close to his chest.

> Instead of smelling a rat, the teachers' unions paddled towards their doom with the naïveté of a new bride outside Dracula's castle.

> The policy is a hot potato that could leave the Government with egg on its face.

Other techniques

HYPERBOLE

Hyperbole is exaggeration for the sake of emphasis (as in *I'm fearfully sorry*), often for comic effect:

> *I have had occasion, I fancy, to speak before now of these pick-me-ups of Jeeves's and their effect on a fellow who is hanging to life by a thread on the morning after ...*

> *For perhaps the split part of a second nothing happens. It is as though all Nature waited breathless. Then, suddenly, it is as if the Last Trump had sounded and Judgement Day set in with unusual severity.*

> *Bonfires burst out in all parts of the frame. The abdomen becomes heavily charged with molten lava. A great wind seems to blow through the world, and the subject is aware of something resembling a steam hammer striking the back of the head. During this phase, the ears ring loudly, the eyeballs rotate, and there is a tingling about the brow.*

> *And then, just as you are feeling that you ought to ring up your lawyer and see that your affairs are in order before it is too late, the whole situation seems to clarify. The wind drops. The ears cease to ring. Birds twitter. Brass bands start playing. The sun comes up over the horizon with a jerk.*

> *And a moment later all you are conscious of is a great peace.*
>
> (P.G. Wodehouse, *Right Ho, Jeeves*)

> *But there he was, always, a steaming hulk of an uncle, his braces straining like hawsers, crammed behind the counter of the tiny shop at the front of the house, and breathing like a brass band; or guzzling and blustery in the kitchen over his gutsy supper, too big for everything except the great black boats of his boots. As he ate, the house grew smaller; he billowed out over the furniture, the loud check meadow of his waistcoat littered, as though after*

a picnic, with cigarette ends, peelings, cabbage-stalks, birds'
bones, gravy; and the forest fire of his hair crackled among the
hooked hams from the ceiling.

(Dylan Thomas, *A Prospect of the Sea*)

Exaggerated metaphors and similes play their part in both
passages, and in the second of them extra emphasis is provided by
initial consonants repeated insistently (*breathing like a brass band*,
black boats of his boots) – see the section on alliteration below.

Imagery ought not to draw attention to itself, otherwise writing
becomes too contrived and artificial. However, this objection does
not apply to writing where a larger-than-life or artificial element is
deliberate, as it is for comic purposes in the passages just quoted.

PERSONIFICATION

Personification is ascribing human attributes to inanimate things:

> All Nature waited breathless.

> The shop doors yawned and the windows blinked in the
> afternoon haze.

PARADOX

A paradox is a statement that appears self-contradictory but
contains a truth:

> The child is father to the man.
> Cowards die many times before their death.

UNDERSTATEMENT

Understatement is the use of a consciously restrained tone.
The motive may be modesty, humour or good manners:

> rather unnerving (*terrifying*); tired and emotional (*drunk*);
> misunderstanding (*blunder*)

IRONY

Irony is saying the opposite of what you mean while making it clear what you do mean. A person who speaks ironically (for example, saying 'That was clever' to someone who has just done something foolish) expresses the real meaning by an ironical tone of voice. A person who writes ironically must signal the fact clearly if the irony is to be detected; if it is not, serious misunderstanding will occur.

> ### Insight
>
> It is a delight to savour pure unadulterated irony where you have to look behind the words to find the writer's standpoint: the early songs of Randy Newman, for instance – is *Short People* really an attack of people of limited height?
>
> However, misunderstanding is certainly possible. Jonathan Swift's miniature masterpiece, *A Modest Proposal*, has sometimes shocked people in the wrong way as a justification of cannibalism. In it he coolly proposes the killing and eating of Irish infants as of great benefit to all. The reader has to supply the moral stance (eating people is wrong) and the political viewpoint (the people are the riches of a country, according to the then current Mercantilist theory) to see that it is a coruscating attack on the treatment of the Irish.

Irony derives its richness from having a double meaning, an apparent one and a camouflaged one, sometimes finely balanced. Its usefulness is that it allows a writer to make a judgement on his subject without being direct or heavy-handed (*That was clever* is a judgement very different in its effect from *That was stupid*).

Discussing MPs' official visits to foreign parts, Simon Hoggart writes,

> *Naturally, fact-finding visits are very important. It is essential that our legislators are acquainted with the latest situation*

> *regarding tea prices in Ceylon, aircraft spares in Los Angeles,*
> *political unrest in the Caribbean, Common Market support for*
> *olive oil producers in Sicily, and the dangers in skiing holidays at*
> *St Moritz. Now and again they go somewhere unpleasant too,*
> *but this is usually tacked on to an urgent mission to some more*
> *agreeable and sunny clime.*
>
> (On the House)

There is irony in the inclusion of *skiing holidays at St Moritz*
alongside *aircraft spares*, *political unrest* and *Common Market
support*. The final sentence, however, reveals that the whole list has
a certain irony and that all the visits are perhaps not as *important*
as we were originally led to believe.

Irony in fiction is more usually a matter of prevailing tone or viewpoint
than of occasional technique, but something of its flavour is seen in this
extract from Malcolm Bradbury's *Who Do You Think You Are?*

> *But it was good to be near the city centre, to see the new*
> *sky-scraper blocks rising, the neon flashing, the ambulances*
> *roaring, the rattle of terrorist explosions, the pulse and throb*
> *of modern urban living. They moved through the new Bull Ring,*
> *the new underpasses, the multi-storey car-parks, the concrete*
> *complexities of New Street station; Edgar was frequently at New*
> *Street station, because he had constantly to travel up to London,*
> *on the Inter-City, to sit on committees, see his publisher, advise*
> *reform groups, take part in a demo, do a television programme.*
> *He was not a narrow academic; and he had arranged his teaching*
> *timetable at the university so that he could have one free day a*
> *week to keep up in the world.*

The straight-faced equation of skyscrapers, neon lights and
ambulances with *the rattle of terrorist explosions* as equally
authentic parts of *the pulse and throb of modern urban living* is
little more than a cynical joke; but the later equation of *seeing
a publisher* or *doing a television show* with *taking part in a
demonstration* tells us that Edgar views these activities as equally
important and may suggest that the author regards this view, or

all these activities, with amusement, given that regularly attending demos suggests habit rather than sincerity.

ALLITERATION

Alliteration is the repetition of the same consonants:

> Children cheering and clapping.
> Light-fingered ladies looking longingly at the lingerie.
> Mean, moody and magnificent.
> Scorched sons of the sea sitting stolidly on the seawall.

Alliteration makes words easier to remember. This is why advertisements and jingles on TV, radio, posters, packets, etc., frequently use alliteration, e.g. *Tuttle's Toothpaste Totally Whitens Teeth*, in which the extra 't's in *Tuttles* and *whitens* strengthen the effect.

Tongue twisters, such good fun to say, are based on alliteration:

> She sells sea shells by the seashore.

> Peter Piper picked a peck of pickled peppers
> If Peter Piper picked a peck of pickled peppers,
> Where's the peck of pickled peppers Peter Piper picked?

> There's no need to light a night-light
> On a light night like tonight,
> For a night-light light's a slight light
> When the moonlight's white and bright.

Alliteration can be used for comic effect, as in this passage from Shakespeare's *A Midsummer's Night's Dream*, where Pyramus thinks Thisby is slain:

> **Whereat with blade, with bloody blameful blade,**
> **He bravely broached his boiling bloody breast.**

Have fun with language!

1 *Read again the passages by Lawrence and Golding in Chapter 11. Pick out some similes and some metaphors and consider how they work. How effective are they in their contexts?*

2 *Think up similes or metaphors of your own to describe:*
   a *a hare running round a field*
   b *a ship sailing in to harbour*
   c *your local supermarket on a Saturday morning.*

3 *Think up a slogan for a new breakfast cereal, using*
   a *hyperbole*
   b *alliteration.*

10 THINGS TO REMEMBER

1   A simile is an open comparison, usually begun with as or like, but not always. Words such as than can be used or a simile can be indicated by a longer phrase: ... is similar to ..., perhaps.

2   A metaphor is an implied comparison in which the subject is simply referred to as the object of the comparison.

3   Metaphors can work even more allusively. You don't need to refer to an engine as a wild animal; you can simply say that it roared.

4   Consistency in metaphors and similes is important. A mixed metaphor is fine for comic effect, but not otherwise, and the development of a stream of related comparisons can be very effective.

5   Don't worry if it is sometimes difficult to decide what literary device is being employed: personification, for instance, is a type of metaphor.

6   Irony depends upon opposites. At its simplest it consists of saying the opposite of what you think.

7   There is no ring-fence between literary terms. If you wonder, 'Is it irony or sarcasm?' it's probably both.

8   Ironically is often wrongly used for coincidentally. If you apply for a job and find that your boss is a former colleague, that is a coincidence. However, it would be ironic if you had told all and sundry that he was a hopeless case who would never get promotion!

9 *The irony of situation (dramatic irony) also depends on opposites: a character in a novel relaxes in a pub after escaping great danger, but thanks to the omniscient narrator the reader knows that his arch-enemy is seated at the bar.*

10 *All these figures of speech depend on calculated effect; none should be overdone, unless you make a conscious decision to do so. This particularly applies to alliteration: overdone it becomes a novelty item, a tongue-twister.*

13

Creative writing

In this chapter you will learn:
*   **about writing creatively**.

Whether you have an essay to write or are preparing for an English exam, or whether you have some other form of creative continuous writing to do, there are certain techniques that are helpful to follow; techniques which are best exemplified though published models.

The reader

A fundamental question to be asked every time you sit down to write is, who are you writing for? Your audience is probably a teacher or examiner in most cases, or else an imagined reader. If you write a story or a description, you have pictures in your mind, and thoughts and feelings you want to express. Your readers are like a blank canvas waiting to be filled in with shapes and colours. If you spare them a thought from time to time, as you would a live audience, you are more likely to keep their interest. When putting forward your point of view or discussing a topic, picture them as tolerably intelligent listeners; in that way you are less likely to make the mistake of stating the obvious or treating them like idiots. Better still, if you think of them as unconvinced or even as opposed to your views, you will be stimulated to anticipate their objections and deal with them, so that your treatment of the subject will be more comprehensive, your style sharper and more persuasive. You will be helped and your style will be more natural if you remember that you are writing for an audience, not committing words to the void.

Making a word picture

To make a word picture, a writer needs the sharp observation of precise visual detail. Such detail is found in the passage by Ruth Prawer Jhabvala in Chapter 11. Descriptive writing comes alive when the writer uses all five senses: sound, smell, taste and touch are important to create a feeling of reality, as well as sight. In the following passage the writer gains actuality from using more than just one of his five senses:

So in the ample night and the thickness of her hair I consumed my fattened sleep, drowsed and nuzzling to her warmth of flesh, blessed by her bed and safety. From the width of the house and the separation of the day, we two then lay joined alone. The darkness to me was like the fruit of sloes, heavy and ripe to the touch. It was a darkness of bliss and simple langour, when all edges seemed rounded, apt and fitting; and the presence for whom one had moaned and hungered was found not to have fled after all.

My Mother, freed from her noisy day, would sleep like a happy child, humped in her nightdress, breathing innocently and making soft drinking sounds in the pillow. In her flights of dream she held me close, like a parachute to her back; or rolled and enclosed me with her great tired body so that I was snug as a mouse in a hayrick ...

At dawn, when she rose and stumbled back to the kitchen, even then I was not wholly deserted, but rolled into the valley her sleep had left, lay deep in its smell of lavender, deep on my face to sleep again in the nest she had made my own.

(Laurie Lee, *Cider with Rosie*)

> ## Insight
> The Laurie Lee extract illustrates the appeal to the senses
> referred to above. It also illustrates the use of similes as
> explained in Chapter 12. You should be able to find at least
> three significant similes in the extract – which do you find the
> most effective?

Telling a story

When describing actions, especially violent ones, the stylistic
devices of short sentences, concentration on strong verbs (the
action words), and sparing use of adjectives so as not to slow
down the pace, give the reader the sense of being at the scene and
witnessing what took place. After reading the following passage
from *A Farewell to Arms* by Ernest Hemingway (1899–1961), try
changing the past to the present tense to judge whether or not the
sense of immediacy and excitement is increased:

> *I ducked down, pushed between two men, and ran for the
> river, my head down. I tripped at the edge and went in with a
> splash. The water was very cold and I stayed under as long as I
> could. I could feel the current swirl me and I stayed under until
> I thought I could never come up. The minute I came up I took a
> breath and went down again. It was easy to stay under with so
> much clothing and my boots. When I came up the second time
> I saw a piece of timber ahead of me and reached it and held on
> with one hand. I kept my head behind it and did not even look
> over it. I did not want to see the bank. There were shots when
> I ran and shots when I came up the first time. I heard them when
> I was almost above water. There were no shots now. The piece of
> timber swung in the current and I held it with one hand. I looked
> at the bank. It seemed to be going by very fast. There was much
> wood in the stream. The water was very cold. We passed the
> brush of an island above the water. I held on to the timber with
> both hands and let it take me along. The shore was out of
> sight now.*

In the next passage we see short sentences (and short paragraphs) used for a different purpose: the creation of tension and a sense of danger.

> *The cries, suddenly nearer, jerked him up. He could see a striped savage moving hastily out of a green tangle, and coming towards the mat where he hid, a savage who carried a spear. Ralph gripped his fingers into the earth. Be ready now, in case.*
>
> *Ralph fumbled to hold his spear so that it was point foremost; and now he saw that the stick was sharpened at both ends.*
>
> *The savage stopped fifteen yards away and uttered his cry.*
>
> *Perhaps he can hear my heart over the noises of the fire. Don't scream. Get ready.*
>
> *The savage moved forward so that you could only see him from the waist down. That was the butt of his spear. Now you could see him from the knee down. Don't scream.*
>
> (William Golding, *Lord of the Flies*)

Insight

Tension is created by the short sentences in the passage from William Golding, certainly, but also by a shift in viewpoint during the passage, exemplified by the personal pronouns used. To begin with the author uses the third person, operating as an omniscient narrator: *he* or the proper noun, *Ralph*. At the end of the first paragraph Golding puts in a command, *Be ready now* – Ralph 'speaking' to Ralph, giving a closer identification with the character. In the fourth paragraph *Perhaps he can hear my heart* moves to a first person narrative – Ralph speaking directly to the reader – and then a strange second person narrative – *you could only see ...* – which is an extension of the idea of Ralph-to-Ralph. As a result, the reader is taken much more fully inside Ralph's thinking and shares his fear.

If your aim in a passage of descriptive writing is to screw the tension almost to breaking point, the following example is an excellent model. The dialogue in particular conveys the children's fear. A 13-year-old girl and her 8-year-old brother are the only survivors of an air crash in the middle of the Australian desert:

It was silent and dark, and the children were afraid. They huddled together, their backs to an outcrop of rock. Far below them, in the bed of the gully, a little stream flowed inland – soon to peter out in the vastness of the Australian desert. Above them the walls of the gully climbed smoothly to a moonless sky.

The little boy nestled more closely against his sister. He was trembling.

She felt for his hand, and held it, very tightly.

'All right, Peter,' she whispered, 'I'm here.'

She felt the tension ebb slowly out of him, the trembling die gradually away. When a boy is only eight, a big sister of thirteen can be wonderfully comforting.

'Mary,' he whispered, 'I'm hungry. Let's have something to eat.'

The girl sighed. She felt in a pocket of her frock, and pulled out a paper-covered stick of barley sugar. She broke it, gave him half, and slipped the other half back in her pocket.

'Don't bite,' she whispered, 'Suck.'

Why they were whispering, they didn't know. Perhaps because everything was so silent: like a church. Or was it because they were afraid; afraid of being heard?

For a while, the only sounds were the distant rippling of water over stone, and the sucking of lips round a diminishing stick of barley sugar. Then the boy started to fidget, moving restlessly from one foot to another. Again the girl reached for his hand.

'Aren't you comfy, Peter?'

'No.'

'What is it?'

'My leg's bleeding again. I can feel the wet.'

[At last they fall asleep.]

In the darkness beyond the gully, the bush came slowly to life.

A lumbering wombat came creeping out of his ground den. His short stumpy body forced a way through the underscrub; his long food-foraging snout ploughing through the sandy earth in search of his favourite roots. Suddenly he stopped: sniffed: his nostrils dilated. He followed the strange new scent. Soon he came to the gully. He looked the children over thoughtfully, not hungrily, for he was a vegetarian, an eater of roots. His curiosity satisfied, he shambled slowly away.

Random fireflies zigzagged slowly by; their nightlights flickering like sparkles from a roving toy-sized forge.

Soon, creeping along the edge of darkness, came another creature; a marsupial tiger-cat, her eyes widened by the night to glowing oriflammes of fire. She too had scented the children; she too clambered into the gully and looked them over. They smelt young and tender and tempting; but they were large; too bulky, she decided, to drag back to her mewling litter. On velvet paws she slunk away.

(James Vance Marshall, *Walkabout*)

Another method is to personify the thing described, so giving it life. In the following piece the French fishing boat is treated as a poor stricken female in her death throes:

There, not a hundred yards away and clearly visible in the strengthening light of dawn, was the French crabber. As they

*watched helplessly from the cliff top, the distance between the
drifting boat and the rocks below them dwindled rapidly.*

*Now the crabber was only a few yards from the rocks. One instant
she was prostrated deep in the troughs of the waves, the next she was
flicked up like a cork to their crests. She rolled dementedly from side
to side, her gunwales awash. Her mainmast was shattered at deck
level; her mainsail dragged overboard like an enormous broken
wing. Three of the crew were amidships, clinging to the tangled stays;
the small figure of the cabin boy crouched desperately in the bows.*

*The watchers cried aloud as the boat, with an appalling crash, was
hurled upon the rocks. A jagged hole appeared in her side. Savagely
the waves lifted her and dropped her back again and again upon
the rocks that were goring her. Second by second the wound in her
side grew larger and the water seethed in and out of her body.*

*Another cry from the watchers. The crabber shuddered
backwards, the rocks tearing her side away. For a moment her
bowsprit pointed its accusing finger heavenwards. Then her back
broke. The men amidships vanished as if they had never been.
As her bows crashed forward the watchers looked in vain for the
boy: the sea had swallowed him also.*

(A.R. Ward)

Describing a person

A convincing description of a person calls for acute observation
coupled with imaginative powers. Lifelike characters are created
from observing actual people combined with imaginary people.
Beware of overdoing the detail: concentrate on the points that
distinguish your character from all others, as does Thomas Mann
in this extract from his *Death in Venice*:

*Gustave von Aschenbach was somewhat below middle height, dark
and smooth-shaven, with a head that looked rather too large for his
almost delicate figure. He wore his hair brushed back; it was thin at*

the parting, bushy and grey on the temples, framing a lofty, rugged,
knotty brow – if one may so characterise it. The nose-piece of his
rimless gold spectacles cut into the base of his thick, aristocratically
hooked nose. The mouth was large, often lax, often suddenly
narrow and tense; the cheeks lean and furrowed, the pronounced
chin slightly cleft. The vicissitudes of fate, it seemed, must have
passed over his head, for he held it, plaintively, rather on one side.

Sometimes word portraits of real people are flattering, sometimes
close – often painfully so – to the truth. The portrait is then of a
person, 'warts and all'.

This portrait by Paul Hentzer, a foreigner, of Queen Elizabeth I
(1558–1603) is a truthful one, not at all flattering, yet a favourable
one. The writer achieves his effect by concentrating solely on the
Queen's physical characteristics:

Next came the Queen, in the sixty-fifth year of her age as we were
told, very majestic; her face oblong, fair, but wrinkled; her eyes
small, yet black and pleasant; her nose a little hooked; her lips
narrow, and her teeth black (a defect the English seem subject to,
from their too great use of sugar). She had in her ears two pearls,
with very rich drops. Her hair was of an auburn colour, but false;
upon her head she had a small crown. Her hands were slender, her
fingers rather long, and her stature neither tall nor low. Her air
was stately, her manner of speaking mild and obliging.

One piece of advice often given when making a word portrait of a
person is to exaggerate what is essential to that person. When the
advice is followed, care is needed not to make the exaggeration
too great, unless you are trying for a comic effect. Among the
many details we could describe, we could choose those which, for
example, encapsulate our subject's appearance, distinguishing him
from others. Charles Dickens (1812–1870) was a master of such
selection, as these two quotations show:

He was a rich man: banker, merchant, manufacturer, and what not.
A big, loud man, with a stare, and a metallic laugh. A man made out
of a coarse material, which seemed to have been stretched to make

so much of him. A man with a great puffed head and forehead,
swelled veins in his temples, and such a strained skin to his face that
it seemed to hold his eyes open and lift his eyebrows up. A man with
a pervading appearance on him of being inflated like a balloon, and
ready to start. A man who could never sufficiently vaunt himself a
self-made man. A man who was always proclaiming, through that
brassy speaking-trumpet of a voice of his, his old ignorance and his
old poverty. A man who was the Bully of humility.

... He had not much hair. One might have fancied he had talked
it off, and that what was left, all standing up in disorder, was in
that condition from being constantly blown about by his windy
boastfulness.

(Charles Dickens, *Hard Times*, Book I, Chapter 4)

He was a snub-nosed, flat-browed, common-faced boy enough;
and as dirty a juvenile as one would wish to see; but he had
about him all the airs and manners of a man. He was short for
his age: with rather bow-legs, and little sharp, ugly eyes. His hat
was stuck on top of his head so lightly, that it threatened to fall
off every moment – and would have done so very often, had he
not had a knack of every now and then giving his head a sudden
twitch, which brought it back to its old place again. He wore a
man's coat, which reached nearly to his heels. He had turned
the cuffs back, half-way up his arm, to get his hands out of the
sleeves: apparently with the ultimate view of thrusting them into
the pockets of his corduroy trousers; for there he kept them. He
was, altogether, as roystering and swaggering a young gentlemen
as ever stood four feet six, or something less, in his boots.

(Charles Dickens, *Oliver Twist*, Chapter 8)

Discussing a topic

Discursive writing is writing that seeks to discuss or argue a point of
view. Facts, opinions and arguments will follow one another either
logically or at random, and the writer's aim is achieved when these are

sufficiently interesting to grip the reader's attention. Precise examples, things seen and described, are more telling than abstract argument.

The use of imagery to make abstract ideas more concrete and 'telling' is a powerful tool to use in discursive writing. The poet and religious writer John Donne (1572–1631) uses an extended metaphor to bring home to his readers that we are all members one of another:

> *No man is an island, entire of itself. Every man is a piece of the continent, a part of the main [i.e. the mainland]. If a clod be washed away by the sea, Europe is the less, as well as if a promontory were, as well as if a manor of thy friend's or of thine own were. Any man's death diminishes me, because I am involved in mankind. And therefore never send to know for whom the bell tolls: it tolls for thee.*

> *(Devotions Upon Emergent Occasions, 1624)*

An equally powerful use of extended metaphor to bring home what could have been an abstract argument is this from Miles Coverdale's English Bible:

> *Lay not up for yourselves treasure upon earth, where the rust and moth doth corrupt, and where thieves break through and steal. But lay up for you treasures in heaven, where neither rust nor moth doth corrupt, and where thieves do not break through nor steal. For where your treasure is, there will be your heart also.*

In the following quotation, Joseph Conrad (1857–1924) convinces his readers of the immense age of the earth by describing the sea in a storm, thus bringing to vivid life what could have been a sterile list of facts:

> *If you would know the age of the earth, look upon the sea in a storm. The grayness of the whole immense surface, the wind furrows upon the face of the waves, the great masses of foam, tossed about and waving, like matted white locks, give to the sea*

> *in a gale an appearance of hoary age, lustreless, dull, without*
> *gleams, as though it has been created before light itself.*
>
> (Joseph Conrad, *The Mirror of the Sea*)

A minor way of avoiding the abstract in your discursive writing is
to remove surplus words in such phrases as these:

---

a speech of a controversial *nature* – a controversial speech

work on a voluntary *basis* – voluntary work

in the *majority* of cases, breakages occurred – most breakages
occurred

a certain amount of difficulty – some difficulty

is not a workable proposition – cannot be done

the *nature* of the problem is *such* that – the problem is that

should circumstances arise in which – if

the trend is towards earlier marriages – people are marrying earlier

a more modern *type of* – a more modern

in respect of – about

the extent of the damage – how much damage

complete lack of – no

a greater measure of – more

police *involved in* patrolling – patrolling police

an inadequate level of – low

from an educational standpoint – educationally

a considerable proportion of children – many children

a high degree of support – strong support

an important *factor to take into account* is the weight – the weight
is important

the situation with regard to spare parts is that they are – spare parts
are

there is a good deal of uncertainty in connection with the overall
position – nobody knows what is happening

Reflective writing

Reflective writing usually has two components: a statement of a personal experience, taste or interest, and some reflections or feeling about it. It is particularly important to remember the reader and to avoid being too private, gossipy or self-indulgent.

The more lively your observations, the stronger your enthusiasms and involvement, the greater will be your success in gaining and holding the reader's attention. If you are writing about your enjoyment of something, be bold and enthusiastic in expressing your thoughts and feelings, and how much your enjoyment depends on your senses. Adopt a similar tone when writing about your interests, for example. People enjoy reading about other people's interests.

As in discursive writing, make full use of imagery and specific vivid detail; avoid abstract, vague, colourless statements. If your aim is to convince the reader of something, then your closing argument should be as strong as you can make it. Both the Huxley and Breijer passages in Chapter 11 will repay study as excellent examples of reflective writing in which the authors show their strong and enthusiastic commitment to their subject.

Essay writing

If you are writing for teachers or examiners you should remember that they will be assessing your material on the following criteria:

- ▶ The content: is it interesting, original, fresh, personal, sincere, relevant?
- ▶ The expression: is it lively or dull? is there breadth of vocabulary? is the style fitting?
- ▶ The organization: is there order or logic? a sense of flow? do sentences and paragraphs relate to each other? does the piece

hang together with a bright beginning, a helpful development
and a satisfying conclusion?
▶ Accuracy of spelling, punctuation and grammar.

PARAGRAPHS

It is important to lay out your writing in proper paragraphs.
A paragraph groups together related information and ideas. It also
marks the movement of one topic to another.

Paragraphs may either be indented or, as happens commonly
nowadays, start at the margin, in which case a line space is left
between the end of one and the beginning of the next.

Writers use shorter paragraphs than they once did. The break
between paragraphs provides a welcome relief for the reader's eyes
and attention and also makes the page look less forbidding.

Some writing hints

The raw material of writing consists of the perceptions, feelings,
thoughts, opinions, beliefs, memories, etc., that we all have. The
craft of writing is the organisation of these into coherent form and
shape. Here are a few hints:

▶ Write from personal experience or observation if possible.
▶ In descriptions of people and places select significant detail.
▶ If telling a story, root it in place and time.
▶ Know what the end of your story is before you start; make
  sure it's a good one.
▶ Keep a balance between the story and the setting, atmosphere
  and characters.
▶ Keep a diary or word sketch-book, with jottings of scenes,
  people, events, news items, dreams, mannerisms or gestures,
  etc., to be used at a later date.

10 THINGS TO REMEMBER

1 *In writing be as aware of your audience as you would be in speaking.*

2 *If the reader is to 'feel' what you are writing, it is helpful to appeal to more senses than just sight.*

3 *There is no such thing as the best length for a sentence. You should consider the impact you wish to make; short sentences that might seem over-simple in some situations can work well in dramatic or exciting narrative.*

4 *The figures of speech, such as simile and personification, discussed in Chapter 12, need to be applied with shrewdness and imagination.*

5 *Observation is the key to good descriptive writing.*

6 *Selection of details is crucial to descriptive writing: well chosen to complement each other rather than just piled up in profusion.*

7 *Exaggeration of prominent distinguishing features can effectively characterize an individual, but you must be aware of the effect you are creating: exaggerate too much and the effect is comic or melodramatic – which may, of course, be the effect you seek.*

8 *Paragraphing is a key element of style. It is important to avoid monotony and balance short and long paragraphs.*

9 *In a discursive piece identifying the subject of the paragraph in the first sentence (the topic sentence) is often helpful.*

10 *There is no one blueprint for organization – in an imaginative piece you may even wish to confuse the reader – but it is always worthwhile to consider the organization, even of a piece that attempts to seem disorganized!*

14

Summaries and comprehension

In this chapter you will learn:
- *how to write a summary*
- *about reading comprehension.*

Making a summary

A summary is a brief account giving the main points of a text. Other names for summary are 'précis' and 'abstract'.

The ability to make a summary is well worth developing. It is a skill allied to that of making notes, where all inessential words, including linking words, are deleted, leaving only the bare facts. A summary, however, is a piece of connected prose. Making a summary, and making and taking notes, are part of a student's armoury, saving time and allowing essential facts to be memorized more easily. Providing a summary is also an important part of communication in official and commercial transactions. Someone in a senior position calls for certain matters to be presented uncluttered by supporting evidence or reasoning. A competent summary will meet this demand.

Practice in making a summary is practice in grasping a central thread and separating the wheat from the chaff. It sharpens and strengthens both the powers of concentration and comprehension, and the ability to write in a style appropriate to the occasion.

LANGUAGE AND STYLE

A summary should be in your own words. The language should be objective and impersonal, the important points you are summarizing expressed in as clear and straightforward a style as possible. The aim is to produce the essence of the original text in plain English, freed of illustrative detail or examples.

PREPARATION

Here is a well-tried method:

1 *Quickly read through the passage to ascertain what it is about.*
2 *Reread it slowly and carefully to grasp its exact meaning.*
3 *Underline the essential points.*
4 *Write these down, summarizing them in your own words.*
5 *Check that you have omitted all irrelevant detail, including 'fillers' such as 'in other words', 'on the one hand', and so on.*
6 *Make a word count.*
7 *Write out your summary in plain English.*
8 *Check that nothing of importance has been omitted. If so, make the necessary adjustments.*

Insight

The first essential in making a summary is an example of inaction, of avoiding something. If the original is clearly written, there is a temptation to start your summary in similar words – this temptation must be resisted! The summary will end up as something more like a paraphrase (re-worded at similar length) and this is particularly inappropriate when, as often happens, you are given a word limit for a summary.

PRACTICE

Here is an example:

At a typical football match we are likely to see players committing deliberate fouls, often behind the referee's back, trying to take a throw-in or a free kick from incorrect but more advantageous positions in defiance of the clearly stated laws of the game, and challenging the ruling of the referee or linesman in an offensive way which often deserves exemplary punishment or even sending-off. No wonder spectators fight among themselves, damage stadiums, or take the laws into their own hands by invading the pitch in the hope of affecting the outcome of the match.

(95 words)

Summary

Unsportsmanlike behaviour by footballers deserves severe punishment and causes hooliganism among spectators.

(13 words)

Exercise 1 Make a summary of the following in not more than 140 words:

In the search for good grazing for his beasts, and later when the first corn was planted, primitive man came to realise the importance of rain and sun. In more temperate regions, sun was always more important than rain. So, with eyes on the mysterious sky, where anything could be going on, his first religious instinct was to pray towards the sun.

The moment of the sun's annual rebirth, in late December, was one of the vital religious times of the year. How did people judge this subtle moment, since one does not usually notice any perceptible lengthening of the days until some time later? Living a life close to the elements, tied to one slow place and pace and one set of shadows, it would have been more easily apparent; and priesthoods, whose powers depended on accurate predictions, were vitally interested.

This time of year was also the least laborious on the land. There was time for festivity. Early northern peoples with no exact *astronomical findings began their winter festival earlier, in November, when signs of the sun's recession and scarcity of fodder made necessary the slaughter of a proportion of their cattle. Later, the rites moved to mid-December, either to satisfy whatever more sophisticated organisations built such temples as the sun-orientated Stonehenge, or in sympathy with the imported festivities of a richer Roman period. For the legions brought with them the Saturnalia – a seven-day period of riot and feasting celebrating the birth of Saturn, a legendary King of Italy and farmer of an earlier golden age. His festival was followed without much respite by another, the Kalendae. This was concerned with the date of the new year and the two-faced deity, Janus, god of doorways and spirit of deviousness, who gave his name to the first month. The Persian god, Mithras, who accompanied the Roman soldiery, also celebrated his birth at this time.*

A pre-Christian message of peace and goodwill was a part of these festivities; it was a practical message based on the probability that the usual farmers' battles, which are often disputes about water supply or cattle destroying crops, were in wintry abeyance, and the snow-bound countryside and wintry blizzards kept the warriors around their own fires. So the time of year was one of lighting fires, praising the new sun, relaxation and feasting.

Not until the middle of the fourth century was the birth of Christ officially celebrated at this time. It was a wise, if obvious, decision, for the early Christians were not puritans, and wine and rejoicing were the natural ingredients of the season. If other people were worshipping their gods at the same time it was only naturally competitive for the Christians to worship theirs also; the general atmosphere of rebirth would suggest personal birth.

(Adapted from *Christmas*, by William Sansom)

Follow the same method, or your own adaptation of it, in the following two exercises. Scribble in the margin alterations to your first draft of the most important points, then write your summary in your own words in plain English.

Exercise 2 Make a summary of this article from a broadsheet in not more than 100 words:

Idolising rock stars can be bad for your health
An obsession with Take That or The Spice Girls may be innocent enough when you're 14 years old. Carry the fixation into your twenties, however, and your teen idol can become bad for your health.

Revering famous stars such as Gary Barlow, supermodel Naomi Campbell, or footballer Alan Shearer, into adulthood, increases your chance of psychological problems, eating disorders and problems forming relationships.

'It can be a way of avoiding rather than dealing with problems,' said Dr Tony Cassidy, a psychologist at Nene College, Northampton.

He looked at 163 adults in a pilot study. During adolescence, three-quarters of men and women in the group, now aged between 20 and 28, said they had hero-worshipped someone.

Most people throw off their fixation by their twenties, but Dr Cassidy told the annual conference of the British Psychological Society in Edinburgh that half of those who had idols could not let their feelings go. Those who remained loyal fans tended to be more preoccupied with their weight, and this was particularly true of women. They also disliked their appearance more.

'Another aspect of teen idols is that they serve as models,' said Dr Cassidy. 'Many young girls develop distorted body images of themselves and ultimately eating disorders as a result of the media portrayal of supermodels with ideal bodies.'

The obsessives tend to be less satisfied with their relationships and were more likely to have short-term affairs.

The most extreme fantasised about having a relationship with their adored one or became jealous of their idol's partners.

'It is clear that for many this phase becomes extreme, as was recently demonstrated by a number of attempted suicides among fans of the pop group Take That after the group split up,' he added.

But parents should not rush to the bedroom to rip down their children's posters.

There was one bright spot for fans who did have a teen idol but who gave it up when they reached adulthood – they were subsequently better at problem-solving.

'Having an idol showed a use of imagination which is generally recognised as part of the developmental process,' said Dr Cassidy.

(Glenda Cooper in the *Independent*)

Exercise 3 The article below is an excellent example of sustained irony. Make a summary in not more than 150 words:

Too many 'ologists make you boring

The British Psychological Society, which meets this week in Edinburgh, regularly offers insights which make you wonder about the psychological health of its members. Among this week's astonishing findings are: 'adolescent girls on diets get increasingly miserable as the weeks pass. This is especially true if they see their weight loss goal as hard to reach.' This stunning result of research is by the University of New South Wales in Australia.

People whose teenage obsessions with film or pop stars continue well into adult life may be at risk psychologically. We know this because some psychologists from Northampton have investigated the effects of teen idols on 163 men and women.

If this wasn't enough, we have been further entranced this week by research that suggests that mice given more space, more toys, more food develop better than mice kept in 'poor' homes. Middle-class mice tend to do better than deprived ones.

What is all this information for? Does anyone actually act on it? We are told not to smoke, eat badly or exceed our alcohol units, but we take little notice. The bombardment of expert advice contributes to an increasingly regulatory culture in which those in power impart information to individuals who then ignore it.

This abdication of responsibility has a euphemism – 'increased consumer choice'. Having just returned from the holy land of consumerism, America, I was struck, as always, by what is, despite the mythology, an essentially prohibitive culture. You cannot move for signs and symbols telling you not to do things. You can't cross the road when you want to, have a drink in a bar till you are 21 or visit a urinal without dozens of messages telling you to just say no to drugs.

All this is doubtless the work of experts who however appear to have almost zero insight into human motivation. The one subliminal message that is being conveyed by all these signs is: 'Do as you are told.' Thank God then that we do not do as we are told and that we do not tell experts the truth. This is why opinion polls get things wrong, why psychologists can't see the wood for the trees and why, at a time of supposed excitement, everything feels a bit flat.

Experts live in a universe where control is possible, where knowledge can be handed down from on high and we are supposed to be grateful. They are the only people in the world who believe absolutely what other folks tell them.

Opinion polls, focus groups, psychologists, graphologists, experts on voting patterns are all bearing down heavily upon us. Their understanding of how people work bears little relation to my experience of how we make up our minds, change our minds, lose our minds, or are perfectly able to think two things at once. They would like our behaviour to be as predictable as their banal conclusions. I pray to God we are more exciting than experts give us credit for.

I guess it's up to us. As the old joke about how many therapists it takes to change a light bulb reminds us, it only takes one. But the light bulb has gotta really, really want to change.

(Suzanne Moore, the *Independent*)

Comprehension

No one can make a summary without a thorough understanding of the text. One way often used in examinations of indirectly testing the examinees' powers of comprehension is to ask them to use their summary skills to perform another kind of task.

Exercise 1

For instance, they are requested to write a 200-word letter, using the facts from the accompanying article, to prepare parents of gap-year children for their homecoming and help them to avoid any difficulties that may arise. Obviously, this exercise cannot be done without first making a summary of the text.

Mum, I hardly missed you

(Angela Neustatter reports on the return of the gap-year fledglings)

It was very disconcerting: my breezy breakfast-time conversation induced steely-eyed ennui; chatty revelations about local doings were regarded as the very essence of bourgeois North London preoccupation. Yet my questions about my son's experiences in Zimbabwe (as a volunteer teacher for several months of his post A-level gap year) were treated with contempt – or a sharp riposte about 'not understanding'.

We had swallowed our tears and watched our 18-year-old lad, with his sudden doubts and a premonition of homesickness, go through the departure lounge at Heathrow nine months earlier, but that did not mean the homecoming was a simple and joyful return to the status quo. In truth, in the weeks after he came back there were moments when I felt more than passing empathy with the Carthaginians who in earlier times were wont to sacrifice their first-born son.

That was two years ago. Happily, family life has found its level again, as a close-knit weave of affection and aggravation, discourse and disagreement, in a way I feared might be gone for ever when Zek first returned and seemed so far from us, our values, our way of relating to him.

I can look back now and understand better that it was a time which was confusing and often painful for us – but clearly for Zek too. And once I shared my experience with other gap-returner parents, I realised how familiar it was. Lesley's daughter left home to work in a children's home in Namibia as a giggly sixth-former, both dependent on and rebellious against her mother, and enough of a child for Lesley to feel anxious that she would not cope.

In fact, once Polly got through the first month, during which she felt very lost, she began to enjoy the intimacy she achieved with the children. She felt valued and valuable because of the responsibility she was given. 'Polly found it fantastically difficult to adapt back to our rather quiet life, to what she called our "ghastly consumer values" and to being one of a unit,' Lesley explains. 'She was critical of just about everything. She missed Namibia a lot. In fact, after about three months she had settled down and the maturity she had gained and the sense of her own abilities, which came directly from the gap year experience, were very valuable.'

The mother of Joanna, who went with the GAP organisation to Mexico, echoes this. 'We were desperate to have Jo back and I wanted to be there for her, to let her know I was interested, but actually Jo needed to get her head together and adjust. I didn't understand at first, but now she is able to accept that everyone's lives are different and we find ourselves bandying around clichés like "it's been a life-changing experience".'

Tony Stephens runs the Daneford Trust, a London-based charity which organised Zek's placement and is particularly keen to help children from less privileged homes raise sponsorship money and take up gap-year placements. He hears about problems after the return both from parents, and also from youngsters. 'A good 60 per cent of kids say it's hard settling back again; that's not surprising when you consider that for the first time they have had a wealth of experience which has nothing to do with home, nothing in common with their parents' lives, and of course they have trouble reconciling them.

'These kids arrive back tired, excited, dead pleased with themselves. They've done something fairly momentous but it can be hard getting people to understand the amazement at the way they bathed, coped with stomach upsets, all that. All they hear is a preoccupation with Aunt Jemima's doings and their family's life may seem very small and alien.'

Stephens adds: 'It's understandable that parents feel upset and offended if their child isn't thrilled to be home when they have been so missed, but I urge them to try to understand and just be there as a background, because children certainly do need them.' We have been able to see that over the past couple of years; but I feel for many families whose children have recently returned and who are reeling, as we did, from realising that the child that was so missed has returned as someone other: a young adult with a kit-bag of experiences all of his or her own – and an attitude problem.

But we would do well to let go of our dreams and allow the new person a space, because you can find there's a rather stimulating and enjoyable character in place of the kid who went away.

(The *Guardian*)

Exercise 2

Here is a similar test of comprehension and summary-making skills. Examinees are asked to imagine they are students attending each of the three schools described below. It is their first day, and they are to describe their thoughts and feelings. Make a draft summary about one-third the length of each passage.

1 Diet at Christ's Hospital, a famous boarding school, about 1800

Our breakfast was bread and water, for the beer was too bad to drink. The bread consisted of the half of a three-penny loaf, according to the prices then current. This was not much for growing boys who had nothing to eat from six or seven o'clock the preceding evening. For dinner we had the same quantity of bread, with meat only every other day, and that consisting of a small slice, such as would be given to an infant three or four years old. Yet even that, with all our hunger, we very often left half-eaten – the meat was so tough. On the other days we had milk-porridge, ludicrously thin; or rice-milk, which was better. There were no vegetables or puddings. Once a month we had roast beef; and twice a year (I blush to think of the eagerness with which it was looked for!) a dinner of pork. One was roast, and the other boiled, and on the latter occasion we had our only pudding, which was of peas. I blush to remember this, not on account of our poverty, but on account of the sordidness of the custom. There had much better be none. For supper we had a like piece of bread, with butter or cheese, then to bed, 'with what appetite we might'.

(Leigh Hunt, 1784–1859)

2 David Copperfield surveys the classroom of his new school, Salem House

I gazed upon the schoolroom into which he took me, as the most forlorn and desolate place I had ever seen. I see it now. A long room with three long rows of desks, and six of forms, and bristling all round with pegs for hats and slates. Scraps of old copy-books and exercises litter the dirty floor. Some silkworms' houses made of the same materials are scattered over the desks. Two miserable white mice, left behind by their owner, are running up and down in a fusty castle made of pasteboard and wire, looking in all the corners with their red eyes for anything to eat.

A bird, in a cage very little bigger than herself, makes a mournful rattle now and then in hopping on her perch, two inches high, or dropping from it, but neither sings nor chirps. There is a strange unwholesome smell upon the room, like mildewed corduroys, sweet apples wanting air, and rotten books. There could not be more ink splashed about it, if it had been roofless from its first construction, and the skies had rained, snowed, hailed, and blown ink through the varying seasons of the year.

(Charles Dickens, 1812–1870, *David Copperfield*)

3 My new comprehensive school

I have been attending this new comprehensive school since it opened five months ago, and it is not like any other school I have been in.

I feel like a match in a box, exactly the same as all the other matches. There is hardly any variation in the designs of the buildings, they are all white, and all square or oblong. All the five house blocks are also exactly the same, with off-white walls and ceilings, white paintwork, brown doors with shiny smooth metal handles and a narrow pane of glass in them. The same goes for the teaching blocks. The three enormous gyms are also similar in design to each other, though I must say they are lovely to do things in and there is so much equipment.

The practical block is the only one that differs from the rest. On the first floor are the Commerce Rooms, the Art and Craft Rooms, and a whole lot of Metalwork, Woodwork and Drawing Rooms for the boys. They even also have an Engineering Shop. On the second floor are some Housecraft Rooms, some Needlecraft Rooms, and some laboratories. On the top floor again there are Housecraft and Needlecraft Rooms and some more laboratories.

The school will look better in the summer with the grass a nice green and the flowers and the trees in bloom and the rose bushes. I like the design of the gardens. Most of the buildings are easy to *get to from one another when it is dry, but when it's raining one can get drenched running from one block to another as there is no shelter.*

Another very good thing is the food. We eat our dinners in our house blocks. The food comes through the hatch and is always lovely and hot. There is a choice of menu and everything our cook prepares is very tasty. I like sausage and mash with the delicious gravy, and mince and chips and peas. The sweets are also very nice.

The luckiest children are the first and second years. They will get to know all the teachers and make good use of the excellent buildings and equipment. It is difficult for us fourth years as the P.E. blocks and S block have only lately been finished and ready for use. I should like to stay on, but I have to leave very soon at Easter to earn some money to help my parents. Some of my mates are staying on and they will get great advantages and be happy.

(Susan Ingleton)

Insight

The Susan Ingleton extract is a particularly interesting piece to respond to. Whereas Leigh Hunt and Dickens both write of a time and a school very different from our experience, Susan Ingleton writes of a half-familiar time. The comprehensive school she describes shares much with schools today, but she is clearly writing about the 1960s or 1970s, the days before the raising of the school leaving age when the older fourth years (Year 10) could leave at Easter. A response to this would effectively balance the familiar with the unfamiliar and convey her surprise at things that now seem routine.

Have fun with language!

Write the 200-word letter mentioned in Exercise 1 on page 179.

Write the three imaginative accounts asked for on page 182.

10 THINGS TO REMEMBER

1 *A summary requires the reader firstly to identify the essential points of the original.*

2 *Note-making is an allied activity, but a summary differs by being a piece of continuous prose.*

3 *Skills required for (or learned from) summary include the ability to express yourself clearly, without any unnecessary phrases or fillers.*

4 *As such summaries are not only useful in themselves, but as training in avoiding tautology and vagueness.*

5 *You cannot expect to reproduce the tone of the original, as in the ironic piece by Suzanne Moore.*

6 *A summary is an objective piece of writing.*

7 *The ability to summarise is a worthwhile skill in itself, but most useful when it is employed for some specific purpose.*

8 *While a summary as such is always objective, this specific purpose may require the writer to adopt a certain role, as in the expert writing to parents of gap-year students.*

9 *The activities based on schools are typical of the uses of summary. The final result is a piece of imaginative writing, but one based on effective comprehension and summary.*

10 *Traditionally comprehensions in school have consisted of a passage followed by short questions. However, comprehension simply means 'understanding' and comprehension skills can be tested in many ways, including summary.*

15

Letter writing

In this chapter you will learn:
- *how to write official, business, and personal letters*
- *about email language*
- *about formal invitations and job applications.*

Official and business letters

The increasing use of telephones and computers means that letter writing is far less common than it used to be. Even so, everyone will have to write one from time to time: an application for a job, a reply to a formal invitation, a note of thanks or condolence, an enquiry to a school, business or tax office.

STANDARD FORMAT

The standard format for a business letter is as follows:

	35 Lyndhurst Avenue Exeter EX2 4PA	Address
	20 August 2009	Date
	The Manager	Name and
	Central Bank plc	address of
	Exeter	addressee
	EX6 BX3	
	Dear Mr Stevens	Form of greeting (salutation)
Heading	Deposit A/c 11985	
	Thank you for your letter, ref: WS/RU,	Body of
	of 15 August, inviting me to come and	letter
	see you on Wednesday 25 August at	
	10 a.m. I am pleased to accept and	
	look forward to seeing you.	
Form of ending (subscription)	Yours sincerely	
Signature	*A. L. Harry*	
	(A.L. Harry)	Name printed in brackets

The address

The address may be written or typed with a straight left-hand margin or staggered:

35 Lyndhurst Avenue
  Exeter
    EX2 4PA

20 August 2009

Both are acceptable. So is the address written or typed along the top of the letter, as in the example.

35 Lyndhurst Avenue Exeter EX2 4PA

Note that the address is unpunctuated: punctuation marks have long been dropped. Do not write your name at the top of your letter above

your address, as it will appear at the bottom. If you wish to include
your telephone number and email address, insert under your address:

35 Lyndhurst Avenue
Exeter
EX2 4PA
Tel: 01392 323767
Email: aharry@compuserve.com

The name and address of the person to whom the letter is directed
is needed only in a business letter. A large organization will receive
a large number of letters opened and sorted in a central office. The
inclusion of the addressee's status (manager, etc.) and name will
ensure your letter gets to the right desk quickly.

The letter

Write 'Dear So-and-so' (the name of the addressee), as shown,
against the left-hand margin. Address the person by name if
possible, even though you may never have met. When you address
the letter to a named person, end with 'Yours sincerely'. When you
use only his or her status, end with 'Yours faithfully'. If the name
is not known, use 'Dear Sir', 'Dear Madam' (or 'Dear Sir/Madam'
if the gender is unknown), 'Dear Sirs' (for a company). Less formal
are 'Dear Headmaster', 'Dear Headmistress', 'Dear Editor', 'Dear
Town Clerk'. You will be able to judge when these are appropriate.
Members of a society or club may be addressed semi-formally by
either 'Dear Member' or 'Dear Colleague'.

Dignitaries may be addressed as 'Dear Lord Mayor', 'Dear Lady
Mayoress', 'Dear Bishop', 'Dear Lady Rankworthy', or more
formally as 'Your Worship', 'Most Reverend Sir', 'My Lord'.
On the envelope, however, put the full style and titles:

Professor the Lord Smith of Plymouth
The Fountain
Grant Road
Plymouth
PL6 8EB

The heading (Deposit A/c 11985) is needed only in business correspondence. It enables the appropriate file to be found without first having to read the whole letter, and the letter to be passed to the person best placed to deal with it.

Insight

The form of letters has changed in many details in recent years: in particular, many commas and full stops have tended to disappear. Few people now write 'Mr.' or 'Mrs.', but it is not wrong to do so, simply rather old-fashioned. It is, however, wrong to write 'Miss.' as there is no abbreviation involved. Similarly it is acceptable to write '35, Lyndhurst Road,' – the essential thing is to be consistent, scattered commas merely confuse.

The other major change is that the overwhelming majority of letters are now word-processed, with very beneficial effects. This has brought changes in layout, but the essential rules remain. For instance, addresses may shift from their traditional position, but the rule about not including the sender's name remains. (Of course, a firm's letter headings still carry the company's name.)

Common practice now is to begin the letter itself against the margin, as shown in the example. (Note that no comma is needed after the person's name.) Other paragraphs are not indented and are marked by leaving a space between one and the next. It is not wrong to follow the name with a comma, and to indent paragraphs to separate one from another. In your letters, use whichever style you prefer. Similarly, you may write the ending and your name on the left, as in the example, or on the right. Only 'Yours' needs a capital. Remember it shows possession by its form without an apostrophe. No comma is needed after 'sincerely' or 'faithfully', as in the example, but you may use one if you wish.

The signature in business and formal letters consists of initials and surname, or less formally, forenames and surname.

Women often write Mrs (no full stop), Ms or Miss in brackets after their signature, so that a reply may be appropriately addressed. In case a signature is unreadable, as it often is, the name is printed or typed underneath the signature. In business letters, the signatory's position is typed underneath the typed name: Sales Executive, Personnel Manager, Hon. Treasurer.

When a secretary signs for the person who has dictated the letter, the form adopted is:

G.V. Brown
for Managing Director

I.S. Chambers
for Sales Manager

Points to bear in mind

The appearance of a letter is important. Ensure that there is a pleasing balance between the size and shape of the paper and what is written on it. If a letter is short, do not crowd it all into the top third of the writing paper. Spread the contents carefully, allowing generous margins top and bottom, and left and right. If the letter is long, don't crowd the page with the signature, etc. crammed at the bottom. Use the next page, making sure that some lines appear, rather than just the signature. A letter should be a pleasure to look at, as well as to read. Use a good quality paper and this will add to the pleasure.

STYLE

With the exception of personal letters to family and friends, letters are transactional: making arrangements, giving or requesting information, lodging a protest, responding to points in another letter. The virtues of transactional English – clarity, accuracy, relevance – should be used, otherwise the letter will be too long. Questions should be accurately framed, information complete and specific. Goodwill is lost if the recipient has to spend time puzzling out what the writer means.

Short clear paragraphs are essential: one major point to each. Long paragraphs and jumbled points make it difficult for the recipient to make the reasoned reply the writer desires.

Politeness costs nothing. Strong feelings may be effectively expressed in dispassionate language with rational arguments or an unemotional statement of the facts as the writer sees them. Such an approach will be more effective than tones of outrage, larded with accusations and speculations, especially if the reader has personally committed no offence. Righteous indignation does not go down well and will probably evoke an equally hostile or at least unsatisfactory reply.

Shun technical language or the jargon of your trade unless writing to someone who understands it. Avoid the lifeless jargon that can often be found:

Jargon	Preferred form
Enclosed please find herewith	We enclose
We are in receipt of	Thank you for
I would advise you	(Leave out)
For your information	(Leave out)
We would respectfully request that you	Would you please
The goods were forwarded per post	We posted the goods
I beg to inform you that	(Leave out)
Reference your letter	In response to your letter
It is much regretted that	We are sorry
At your earliest convenience	As soon as possible

Insight

Avoiding jargon is always a good idea. However, in the case of a letter, there are still formulas which are relevant and helpful: making clear what you are sending or what you are responding to, for instance. Formulaic as it is, it is often helpful to start a business letter with 'Thank you for your letter dated ... ' or 'I write with reference to ... ' and, bearing in mind the possibility of contents being separated in the recipient's office, you are always well advised to state, 'I (we) enclose ... '

Finally, check the finished letter to ensure it meets all the above points. Edit and rewrite if you are not satisfied.

All the above points can be summed up by the motto of the Plain English Campaign: Be short, be simple, be human.

Personal letters

Personal letters to family and friends are written in ways you know will interest and please the receiver. There are times, however, when special care is needed when writing letters of condolence or apology, or when writing to someone you don't know well or contact often. The tone on such occasions must be exactly right if the intended effect is to be achieved. Patching up a quarrel is one occasion that needs special care.

There are, however, no rules about layout in a personal letter. You need to put your full address only if the recipient doesn't know it and the greetings at the beginning and end of the letter can be as formal or as affectionate as you wish.

Email language

As anyone who receives emails knows, the language used is very different from that of an 'ordinary' letter. The conventions and punctuation of good English go out of the window. It is quite normal to start with 'Hi' rather than 'Dear so-and-so', to have sentences that don't begin with capital letters, even to use lower case for the word 'I'. It is the type of writing that mirrors speech most closely, and perhaps for that reason it is now immensely popular. The purist might lament its eccentricities, but it is undoubtedly here to stay.

Insight
Email etiquette continues to shift. For example, increasingly, formal letters, job applications, etc., are also being sent this way – and, in these cases, the old niceties still, to an extent,

prevail, so here's a little warning. Don't assume that, because you're using email, a matey colloquialism is in order – it may lose you the job!

Formal invitations

These are often worded impersonally:

> Mr and Mrs R.D. Whittaker
>
> request the pleasure of your company
> at the marriage of their daughter, Jane,
> to Mr Andrew Gray
> at St Christopher's Church, Coulson,
> on Saturday, 9th October, at 3 p.m.
> and afterwards at the Swan Hotel, Wigley
>
> RSVP

The conventional reply is worded similarly impersonally, and sent without salutation or signature.

> 15 Simons Way
> Brackley
>
> 4th September 2009
>
> Mr and Mrs Threlkeld thank Mr and Mrs R.D. Whittaker for their kind invitation to Jane's wedding on Saturday 9th October, and will be very happy to accept.

A similarly formal reply is used when the invitation comes from civic dignitaries or firms.

Job applications

If details of how to reply are given in the advertisement, then follow them. If not, then send:

- ▶ A CV (curriculum vitae or potted biography). Set out your personal details: full name; date of birth; address and telephone number; nationality; education and qualifications; previous relevant experience (job and other); referees (persons to whom enquiries about you can be made). Choose your referees carefully. They should be persons whom you can trust and who have a sound knowledge of you, your character and your achievements. You should always ask your referees beforehand, so that they can be warned. Take care to ensure that other details, personal interests, hobbies and sports, are given if asked for.
- ▶ A letter of application. This is a formal letter and should include relevant information not submitted in your CV, such as your interest in the job and your reasons for applying. Be as brief as possible without being abrupt or terse.

Open testimonials, written by a friend, acquaintance or previous employer and handed to you for future use, are of little value and generally carry little weight. Do not include them in your application unless specifically requested. Nearly all employers prefer confidential references supplied by your referees, but not seen by you.

Have fun with language!

1 *Practise the standard format for a business letter by writing to the local bank about opening an account.*
2 *Write a business letter to a local store complaining about something you recently bought.*
3 *Write a letter to your local council congratulating them on their success in their campaign to make the streets cleaner and tidier.*

10 THINGS TO REMEMBER

1   *While the rules for formal letter writing are still quite strict, it is acceptable to begin even a business letter with 'Dear Simon' or 'Dear Catherine'.*

2   *Business letters are often placed within an ongoing correspondence and will circulate within offices minus their envelopes.*

3   *The relevant information about your address, the person you are writing to, reference numbers and previous letters should be included.*

4   *The incidentals of business letters (punctuation particularly) have been simplified in recent years. It is possible, though unusual, to make use of commas and full stops in the old way.*

5   *Business letters are usually written to achieve a result; adopt a formal clear style, present any necessary evidence and avoid digressions.*

6   *Some firms and professions still adopt jargon in their correspondence. There is no need to follow suit.*

7   *For the 'in-between' stage of a non-formal, semi-personal letter (to relatives you hardly know, perhaps) it is worth remembering that 'Dear Charlotte' is followed by 'Yours sincerely' just as 'Dear Sir' is followed by 'Yours faithfully'.*

8   *Emails can be as formal or as informal as the situation warrants. When the relationship and the situation are to do with business, not friendship, a certain formality is still helpful.*

9   *As always, paragraphing matters. Your chances of a refund, a grant or a job will be improved if the recipient can follow your argument clearly.*

10 *Always keep an updated CV on file.*

16

Report writing

In this chapter you will learn:
- *how to prepare for and write different types of report*
- *about minutes and agendas*.

Many people have to write reports as part of their job, and being able to write a good one is a skill well worth acquiring. A report is usually written to provide someone with information. The person who writes the report will know more about the topic than the person for whom it is written. The writer needs to bear this fact in mind and be sure to present the report in clear and simple English.

Often a report is written for someone in a senior position by someone in a more junior position. The latter will be given time to explore the subject adequately. The writer should take care to strike a balance between the brevity a busy reader will expect and the provision of enough detail to allow the reader to understand, form an opinion, and make the necessary decisions. Knowing the reader and his or her likely responses and requirements makes the task of writing an appropriate report all the easier.

Preparation

The essential first step is to have a clear idea of the purpose of the report. Is it simply to state facts, or persuade, present options, set out pros and cons with or without recommendations, criticize an existing report, evaluate a state of affairs, set out a line of action to be followed? Is the report to be read by one person only, discussed by a committee, circulated for the guidance of others, published to attract comment? The answers to these questions will determine the manner in which the report is written and set out.

A standard report

The components of a standard report are these in the order given:

Title This should be short and to the point.

Purpose A statement of what the report is intended to achieve. The writer's terms of reference may have been prescribed or self-determined. These terms should be laid out at this stage as a useful reminder, both to reader and writer.

Method A description of the method the writer has followed while compiling the report. If the writer's remit is merely to list necessary facts and draw conclusions, there will be no need for this section. If research has been carried out, or a questionnaire circulated, sources and working methods have to be described, because they are the basis of the report's authority. Readers are unlikely to be persuaded by a report's conclusions unless they are able to evaluate how the information has been gathered and treated.

Body of the report The facts and information asked for. The order in which these are set out depends on the content: a chronological order for a series of events; a logical order for an argument; a methodological order for a series of facts, rather than a haphazard order.

Conclusions This is the most important part of a report, and perhaps the only section that will be read. At this stage, the writer should reread the terms of reference and ensure that the conclusions and recommendations cover all the issues.

The report is usually signed and dated.

Longer reports

These may run to many pages and will usually include additional features:

Table of contents This may be set out as in the table of contents at the front of a book.

Summary A summary of the findings, conclusion and recommendations, with cross-references to the main body of the text comes here at the beginning of the report as a separate section. This enables a reader who is interested in only a part of the report, or who does not wish to be concerned with detail, or who wishes to know the report's findings before deciding to read the whole, to get at the information needed.

Appendices When a report has to contain supporting material such as statistical tables, graphs, or quotations from other documents, these are assembled in appendices at the back of the report. They can also come at the bottom of the page as footnotes. The choice depends on the kind of material handled. One objection often made to footnotes is that they distract attention from the main text, especially when they run over from the bottom of one page to the next.

Bibliography A bibliography of the sources consulted – books, articles, witnesses, etc. – provides further evidence of authenticity, and allows interested persons to read further.

Report layout

The way a report is presented – its layout – makes for ease of reading and reference.

NUMBERING POINTS

Numbering of points, use of bold, different fonts, point sizes and spacing are all useful devices:

9 Causes of flooding

In addition to exceptionally high rainfall during July and the following holiday months, and the reduction in industrial demand for water, two contributory factors have been identified.

9.1 The first factor was …
9.2 The second factor, by far the more important, was …
9.3 Other suggested causes have been investigated, but …

TAKING NOTES

A report, or part of it, may have to be based on notes made at a meeting, an interview, a visit of inspection, and so on. Always make the notes as full as possible. A sketchy note can make sense at the time of taking, but may well mean nothing later. Details that seemed unimportant at the time may well turn out to be of some importance later, and a full note would have included them.

When taking notes at a meeting, do not hesitate to interrupt if you are not clear about what was said or agreed. A good chairperson will ensure that every item under discussion is brought to a firm conclusion; a bad chairperson will have to be prompted. In formal meetings, propositions, amendments and resolutions must be recorded verbatim, word for word.

Insight

While the above advice about note-taking is valuable, it is perhaps slightly optimistic about the quality and approachability of the chair of the meeting. Taking suitably thorough notes under pressure is a useful skill. Obviously those skilled in shorthand are at an advantage, but it is helpful for others to devise their own shorthand, maybe based around set abbreviations ('imp' for importance, 'educ' for education), the accepted symbols for regularly used terms like 'therefore' and 'however' and your own symbols for words that occur regularly in the meeting (possibly such words as 'replied', 'disagreed', 'rejected' and so on).

Notes should be written up in continuous prose as soon as possible. This gives the writer the opportunity to prune irrelevancies, unimportant or digressive statements, as well as checking the coherence of the whole. Where necessary, this could be treated as a draft and revised. The normal criteria for transactional writing – clarity, accuracy, brevity, simplicity – apply.

Sometimes all that is necessary is to rearrange the notes in logical order with headings, and using the other devices mentioned above.

STYLE

The report should be written in a formal, impersonal style; little or no use should be made of 'I' or 'We'. Stylistic idiosyncrasies should be avoided. Objectivity and authority are strengthened by omitting such phrases as 'I think' or 'We conclude'. Personal judgments have to be offered when asked for in the terms of reference, and 'I' is perfectly appropriate. Quotations from people should be enclosed in quotation marks, as should quotations from documents, which should be followed by the details of the source: author, title, publisher, publication date and pages should be listed in brackets, or as a footnote, for example:

H. Spooner and R. Tweed, *Flood Prevention* (HMSO 1997), pp. 171–3.

Further references to the same work need only the authors' names, for example:

Spooner and Tweed, p. 64.

Agendas and minutes

If you are the secretary of a local society, club, or group, you will have to prepare the agendas and write up the minutes of meetings. There are certain formalities to be observed.

An **agenda** is a list of business to be transacted, and is sent out to the members with the letter announcing when and where the meeting is to take place. The agenda will be drawn up in consultation with the chairperson. Its purpose is to warn the members of what is to be discussed so that they can prepare themselves. A normal agenda looks like this:

Apologies for absence

Confirmation of the minutes of the previous meeting
(see below)

Matters arising from these minutes

Correspondence

Secretary's report

Named items of business

Any other business (non-agenda items members wish to raise)

Date and time and place of next meeting

Insight

The most important part of the agenda is what is listed above as 'Named items of business'. It is impossible to say how many of these there should be and the nature of them will vary from group to group: from 'Purchase of shed to act as shop' for an allotments committee to 'Preliminary discussion of next season's programme' for a theatre group. What is important, if the chair and secretary are efficient and open, is that matters of real importance are listed here so that members can prepare their views; sliding something in via a crony's intervention under 'Any other business' is not recommended as a way of ensuring a harmonious meeting.

Minutes are the formal record of the proceedings of an organization. Local groups of various kinds elect an executive committee to carry out business on their behalf. Correctly maintained minutes are the evidence that the committee has carried out the business in accordance with the aims and rules of the society. Minutes are also important because they may have legal or financial significance.

Minutes summarize the proceedings in the order of the agenda:

Heading, saying when and where the meeting took place.

Attendance, including apologies for absence. The number present is important: most committees are not permitted to make decisions unless a minimum number of members are present. (This minimum number is called a **quorum.**)

Minutes of the previous meeting Corrections should be recorded, as should the fact that a copy of the minutes was signed by the chairperson after the vote on their acceptance as a correct record, and filed.

Matters arising Notes of any discussions, decisions or actions on any matter raised at the previous meeting.

Correspondence Summaries of correspondence received and replies sent or to be sent.

Reports Briefly summarized. Minutes should always record the committee's approval of any financial transaction for submission to the auditor, whose duty is to check the figures and make sure all expenditure has been legally authorized.

Other items Only important points and decisions need to be recorded. When a discussion is left unfinished, this must be recorded to remind members to pick it up again at the next meeting.

10 THINGS TO REMEMBER

1   *As with so many things in English, good report writing depends in part on identifying the audience.*

2   *A report must carry authority. Therefore, depending on the nature and length of the report, evidence must be clearly presented, whether it be results of a questionnaire, previous volumes cited in a bibliography or charts and tables.*

3   *The people reading the report might be busy, so the conclusions should be clearly laid out – and even, if the report is lengthy, summarized.*

4   *Reports are written in standard English, not notes, but the numbering of statements is often helpful.*

5   *If the report is based upon a meeting or meetings, efficient note-taking is essential.*

6   *Reports are impersonal, so areas of any doubt would be indicated by 'possibly' or 'estimates suggest that', not by 'I think'.*

7   *If you are required to make recommendations, then the first person may be used. It's also useful to indicate clearly in what role you are making these recommendations.*

8   *Agendas for meetings can seem boringly similar to each other and certainly the routine opening items can often be passed over very quickly, but many a meeting has floundered in circular unproductive chat for want of a clear agenda.*

9   *Minutes of meetings require skills already considered such as efficient note-making and summarizing skills (see Chapter 14).*

10 *Remember that register is all-important: the qualities of style required for report writing are very different from those required for creative writing.*

Appendix 1: Irregular verbs

Most verbs form the past tense and past participle by adding *-ed* to the infinitive (*fill – filled*), or *-d* if it already ends in *-e* (*smoke – smoked*). The principal verbs that do not conform to this rule are listed below.

There are three important rules governing the addition of the *-ed* ending.

- ▶ Verbs ending in single vowel + single consonant double the final consonant before *-ed* (*fit – fitted*) unless
  - ▷ the verb has more than one syllable and the accent does not fall on the final one (*falter – faltered*; *benefit – benefited*). Exceptions: *worship – worshipped*; *kidnap – kidnapped*. If the final syllable is stressed, the final consonant is doubled (*commit – committed*; *defer – deferred*). But words ending in single vowel + *l* or *g* double the final *l* or *g* before *-ed* wherever the accent falls (*compel – compelled*; *panel – panelled*). Exception: *parallel – (un)-paralleled*.
  - ▷ the final consonant is *-w*, *-x* or *-y*, which are never doubled.
- ▶ Verbs ending in consonant + *-y* change the *y* to *i* before *-ed* (*copy – copied*).
- ▶ Verbs ending in *-c* add *k* before *-ed* (*panic – panicked*; *traffic – trafficked*; *picnic – picnicked*).

Table of irregular verbs (* = less common form)

Infinitive	Past	Past participle
arise	arose	arisen
awake	awoke (awaked)*	awoken (awaked)*
bear	bore	born (= given birth) borne (= carried, endured; also *borne in mind, borne out,* etc.)
beat	beat	beaten
become	became	become
begin	began	begun
bend	bent	bent
beseech	beseeched (besought)*	beseeched (besought)*
bet	bet	bet
bid	bade, bid	bid, bidden
bind	bound	bound
bite	bit	bitten (bit)*
bleed	bled	bled
blow	blew	blown
break	broke	broken
breed	bred	bred
bring	brought	brought
build	built	built
burn	burnt, burned	burnt, burned
burst	burst	burst
buy	bought	bought
cast	cast	cast
catch	caught	caught
choose	chose	chosen
cling	clung	clung

Infinitive	Past	Past participle
cost	cost (= required payment of)	cost
	costed (= estimated the price)	costed
creep	crept	crept
cut	cut	cut
deal	dealt	dealt
dig	dug	dug
do	did	done
draw	drew	drawn
dream	dreamt, dreamed	dreamt, dreamed
drink	drank	drunk
drive	drove	driven
eat	ate	eaten
fall	fell	fallen
feed	fed	fed
feel	felt	felt
fight	fought	fought
find	found	found
flee	fled	fled
fling	flung	flung
fly	flew	flown
forbear	forbore	forborne
forget	forgot	forgotten
forsake	forsook	forsaken
freeze	froze	frozen
give	gave	given
go	went	gone
grind	ground	ground
grow	grew	grown

(Contd)

Infinitive	Past	Past participle
hang	hung	hung
	hanged (= killed by hanging)	hanged
hear	heard	heard
hide	hid	hidden
hold	held	held
hurt	hurt	hurt
keep	kept	kept
kneel	knelt, kneeled	knelt
know	knew	known
lay	laid	laid
lead	led	led
lean	leant, leaned	leant, leaned
leave	left	left
lend	lent	lent
lie	lay	lain
light	lit (lighted)*	lit (lighted)*
lose	lost	lost
mean	meant	meant
meet	met	met
mow	mowed	mown
pay	paid	paid
quit	quit, quitted	quit
rid	rid	rid
ride	rode	ridden
rise	rose	risen
ring	rang	rung
run	ran	run

Infinitive	Past	Past participle
saw	sawed	sawn
say	said	said
see	saw	seen
seek	sought	sought
sell	sold	sold
send	sent	sent
set	set	set
sew	sewed	sewn, sewed
shake	shook	shaken
shine	shone	shone
shoot	shot	shot
show	showed	shown, showed
shrink	shrank	shrunk
sing	sang	sung
sink	sank	sunk
sit	sat	sat
sleep	slept	slept
sling	slung	slung
slide	slid	slid
slink	slunk	slunk
slit	slit	slit
smell	smelt, smelled	smelt, smelled
sow	sowed	sown
speak	spoke	spoken
speed	sped	sped
	speeded up	speeded up
spell	spelt, spelled	spelt, spelled
spend	spent	spent
spin	spun	spun
spit	spat, spit	spat, spit
split	spilt	split
spread	spread	spread
spring	sprang	sprung
stand	stood	stood
steal	stole	stolen

(Contd)

Infinitive	Past	Past participle
stick	stuck	stuck
sting	stung	stung
stink	stank	stank
stride	strode	stridden
strike	struck	struck
string	strung	strung
strive	strove	striven
swear	swore	sworn
sweep	swept	swept
swim	swam	swum
swing	swung	swung
take	took	taken
teach	taught	taught
tear	tore	torn
tell	told	told
think	thought	thought
throw	threw	thrown
thrive	thrived (throve)*	thrived (thriven)*
tread	trod	trodden, trod
wake	woke (waked)*	woke(n) (waked)*
wear	wore	worn
weave	wove	woven
win	won	won
wind	wound	wound
wring	wrung	wrung
write	wrote	written

Appendix 2: -ible or -able?

The *-ible* ending of adjectives, e.g. *audible*, is found in certain words borrowed from the Latin. It is much rarer than the *-able* ending of adjectives, e.g. *laughable*, found in words of English origin.

The alphabetical list below is of most of the most common *-ible* adjectives. Though you may not need to use many of them, you will be able to consult it when you are in doubt whether to spell an adjective with *-ible* or *-able*. If the adjective you are checking is not in the list, then spell it with *-able*.

accessible
audible

admissible

apprehensible

coercible
combustible
comprehensible
contemptible
corruptible

collapsible
comestible
compressible
convertible
credible

credible
compatible
constructible
corrigible

deductible
destructible
dirigible
dispersible

defensible
diffusible
discernible (or -able)
distendible

descendible
digestible
dismissible
divisible

edible
exhaustible

eligible
extensible

evincible

fallible
forcible

feasible
fusible

flexible

gullible

horrible

(Contd)

illegible	immersible	imperceptible
	impermissible	implausible
impossible	impressible	inaccessible
inadmissible	inaudible	incombustible
incompatible	incomprehensible	incontrovertible
incorrigible	incorruptible	incredible
indefensible	indelible	indestructible
indigestible	indiscernible	indivisible
inedible	ineligible	inexhaustible
infallible	inflexible	ingestible
insensible	insuppressible	insusceptible
intangible	intelligible	invincible
invisible	irascible	irreducible
irrepressible	irresistible	irresponsible
irreversible		

legible

ostensible

perfectible	permissible	persuasible
plausible	possible	

reprehensible	repressible	resistible
responsible	reversible	risible

sensible	submersible	submissible
suggestible	suppressible	susceptible

tangible	terrible	transmissible

unintelligible

vincible	visible